McGraw-Hill Education
500 Review Questions for the MCAT: Biology

D1607550

Also in McGraw-Hill's 500 Questions Series

McGraw-Hill Education

500 Review Questions for the MCAT: Biology

Robert S. Stewart, PhD

New York   Chicago   San Francisco   Athens   London   Madrid
Mexico City   Milan   New Delhi   Singapore   Sydney   Toronto

1 2 3 4 5 6 7 8 9 10   DOC/DOC   1 0 9 8 7 6

ISBN   978-0-07-183614-2
MHID   0-07-183614-4

e-ISBN   978-0-07-183615-9
e-MHID   0-07-183615-2

MCAT is a registered trademark of the Association of American Medical Colleges,
which was not involved in the production of, and does not endorse, this product.

McGraw-Hill Education products are available at special quantity discounts to use as
premiums and sales promotions or for use in corporate training programs.
To contact a representative, please e-mail us at bulksales@mcgraw-hill.com.

ABOUT THE AUTHOR

Robert Stewart, PhD (Norfolk, VA), is a retired U.S. Army officer and currently Professor of Biology and Chair of the Science, Technology, and Mathematics Department at Regent University.

CONTENTS

INTRODUCTION

You've taken a big step toward MCAT success by purchasing *500 Review Questions for the MCAT: Biology*. We are here to help you take the next step and score high on the MCAT so that you can get into the medical school of your choice.

This book gives you 500 multiple-choice questions that cover all the most essential course material. The rationale for each question is clearly explained in the answer key. The questions will give you valuable independent practice to supplement your regular textbook and the ground you have already covered in your classes.

This book and the others in the series were written by expert teachers who know the MCAT inside and out and can identify crucial information along with the kinds of questions that are most likely to appear on the exam.

You may be the kind of student who needs to study extra for a few weeks before the exam for a final review. Or you may be the kind of student who puts off preparing until the last minute before the exam. No matter what your preparation style, you will benefit from reviewing these 500 questions, which parallel the content and degree of difficulty of the questions on the actual MCAT. These questions and the explanations in the answer key are the ideal last-minute study tool for those final weeks before the test.

If you practice with all the questions and answers in this book, we are certain that you will build the skills and confidence you need to excel on the MCAT. Good luck!

—The Editors of McGraw-Hill Education

McGraw-Hill Education

500 Review Questions for the MCAT: Biology

Amino Acids and Proteins

Passage 1: Questions 1–5

Researchers were investigating molecular activity under a variety of environmental conditions. After a series of experiments, the data were used to construct a number of figures, one of which is provided below. However, because of a data stream transmission error, some of the components of the figures were lost, resulting in a scrambling of the figure descriptions and axis scales. Your job is to properly reconstruct and interpret the figures. Please note that one or more options might fulfill the defined criteria as provided.

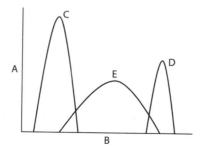

1. One of the experiments dealt with the isolation and characterization of selected enzymes isolated from a newly defined species of archaeobacteria. For this set of data, which of the following would be the most appropriate legend and scale for "A"?

   (A) Enzyme density (ng/mL)
   (B) Relative enzyme activity (mol/sec)
   (C) Reaction product produced (μL/sec)
   (D) System free energy (cal/ng reactants)

2. For the same experiment as in Question 1 dealing with the isolation and characterization of selected enzymes isolated from a newly defined species of archaeobacteria, which would be the most appropriate legend and scale for "B"?

(A) pH (2–9)
(B) Temperature (–40–+60°C) → *beyond enzymatic possibility*
(C) Temperature (70–140°C)
(D) A and C *temp not relevant*

3. One of the experiments dealt with the absorption spectra of isolated photoreactive pigments. For this set of data, which of the following would be the most appropriate legend and scale for "A"?

(A) Percentage absorbance at 400 nm *wavelength would only be 1 point*
(B) Percentage of molecules activated (ng/sec)
(C) Percentage absorbance
(D) Percentage transmittance

4. For the same experiment as in Question 3 dealing with the isolation and characterization of selected photoreactive pigments isolated from a newly defined species of archaeobacteria, which would be the most appropriate legend and scale for "B"?

(A) Energy absorbed (kPa/ng)
(B) Wavelength (300–600 nm)
(C) Percentage absorbance
(D) Emission spectrum (300–600 nm)

5. Given that the scale for "B" includes only visible light from lower to higher energy from left to right, and the scale for "A" measures absorbance, which of the following would be true?

(A) Pigment "C" absorbs red and orange light the least.
(B) Pigment "E" reflects green light the most.
(C) The wavelengths absorbed by pigment "E" most resemble those of chlorophyll.
(D) Pigment "D" absorbs blue light the most.

6. A competitive inhibitor

(A) binds at a site other than the active site.
(B) cannot be processed by the enzyme.
(C) irreversibly binds and inactivates the enzyme.
(D) does not inhibit enzyme activity, but lowers substrate concentration.
(E) binds to and inactivates the substrate.

7. A person with a bacterial infection usually develops a fever. This fever helps protect the person by inhibiting the growth of bacteria because

(A) bacteria reproduce more rapidly at higher body temperatures. *maybe?*

(B) fever blocks the synthesis of proteins in bacteria.

(C) the higher temperature increases the metabolic rate of bacteria.

(D) sweating removes cofactors required by bacteria from the blood.

(E) enzymes do not function as well at temperatures other than that which is optimal.

8. If a small molecule that acts as a substrate for a specific enzyme was modified by being coupled to a larger molecule before the reaction could occur, what would be the most likely result?

(A) The reaction catalyzed by the enzyme would progress in the normal fashion because the part of the molecule that interacts with the enzyme remains substantially unchanged.

(B) The rate of the reaction would increase because of the additional mass of the reactant.

(C) The rate of the reaction would increase because the additional molecular structure would act as a cofactor.

(D) The enzyme would be permanently disabled by the larger portion of the substrate molecule.

(E) The enzyme would not be able to interact with the modified substrate. *wouldn't permanently disable*

9. Complement is a series of blood proteins best associated with

(A) initiation of blood clotting.

(B) regulation of blood clotting.

(C) platelets.

(D) cellular lysis.

(E) apoptosis.

? not sure
complement → cellular lysis

10. If a person undergoes a process whereby selected plasma proteins are removed (plasmapheresis), then that person

(A) is attempting to help someone with chronic infections.

(B) is attempting to help someone with hemophilia.

(C) probably has a chronic infection.

(D) has a large fluid regulatory problem.

(E) is undergoing therapy for leukemia. *?*

take out plasma
remove proteins
plasma back
proteins to someone who needs clotting

11. If a person had a C4 protein deficiency, what problems would they demonstrate?
    (A) Hemophilia
    (B) Recurrent infections
    (C) Frequent episodes of shock
    (D) Pernicious anemia
    (E) Heart arrhythmias

12. If whole blood was collected by venipuncture into a tube containing EDTA or citrate, which of the following could NOT be conducted on the resulting material in the tube?
    (A) Complete blood count
    (B) Hematocrit
    (C) Differential stain
    (D) Quantitation of proteins C3 or C4
    (E) Blood clotting time

13. Which of the following fit within the active site of an enzyme?
    (A) Noncompetitive inhibitors
    (B) Competitive inhibitors
    (C) Coenzyme
    (D) Vitamins
    (E) Cofactors

14. More than 100 amino acids exist in nature. However, only 20 are found in peptides released after ribosomal synthesis. Why is there a difference?
    (A) The unused amino acids are not found in cells.
    (B) The 20 that are used each have two separate R-groups, while the others do not.
    (C) The 20 that are used are the only ones that attach to tRNA.
    (D) The unused amino acids are all D-forms, while the 20 that are used are all L-forms.
    (E) The 20 represent the most ancient forms as seen in the Miller-Urey experiments.

15. What is an "essential" amino acid?
    (A) One that is used most often in protein synthesis.
    (B) One that contributes to essential tertiary structure in proteins.
    (C) One that is used for either initiation or termination of protein synthesis.
    (D) One that must be acquired in the diet of any particular organism.
    (E) An amino acid that is used in protein synthesis, as opposed to one that is not.

16. Which of the following is NOT a way in which organisms use proteins?
   (A) Catalysis
   (B) Storage
   (C) Transport
   (D) Protection
   (E) Micell formation

17. What is the relationship that can be seen when comparing β-pleating with the double helix?
   (A) Both rely on hydrogen bonding to maintain structure.
   (B) Both are synthesized by ribosomes.
   (C) Both contribute to lowered activation energies.
   (D) Both are observed in DNA.
   (E) Both are degraded with the same enzyme.

18. What is the effect of chaperones on proteins?
   (A) They assist in the proper folding of all proteins after synthesis.
   (B) They assure the correct attachment of carbohydrates where needed.
   (C) They prevent the improper aggregation of some proteins under stressful conditions.
   (D) They assist in the formation of disulfide bridges.
   (E) They accompany newly synthesized proteins into endosomes.

19. Identify the following group that contains only hydrophobic amino acids.
   (A) Alanine, leucine, valine
   (B) Glutamine, serine, tyrosine
   (C) Aspartic acid, glutamic acid
   (D) Arginine, histidine, lysine
   (E) Ornithine, homocysteine, homoserine

20. All amino acids contain each of the following attached to the α-carbon EXCEPT
   (A) a carboxyl group.
   (B) a hydrogen atom.
   (C) an amine group.
   (D) a sulfur atom.
   (E) an R–side chain.

21. What, besides the interactions of the various R-groups and the relative charge distribution of the amino acids, helps stabilize the functional three-dimensional structure of a protein?
    (A) Peptide bonds
    (B) Disulfide bridges
    (C) Ionic bonds
    (D) Elevated temperatures
    (E) Lowered temperatures

22. Why do extreme conditions such as an acidic pH or boiling temperatures destroy the normal function of a protein?
    (A) These conditions break disulfide bridges.
    (B) All proteins are denatured at any pH below 4.2.
    (C) Conditions outside of a narrow optimal range alter the tertiary structure of all proteins.
    (D) All proteins are denatured at anything above 45°C.
    (E) These conditions dissociate cofactors required for enzyme function.

23. Why are porin proteins considered integral to a membrane structure rather than merely peripheral and easily removed?
    (A) These proteins covalently bond to the adjacent phospholipids.
    (B) The proteins form stabilizing aggregates within the membrane.
    (C) The spinning nature of the adjacent phospholipids produces vortexing forces that attract the proteins.
    (D) The central portion of the protein is rich in hydrophobic amino acids.
    (E) These proteins are cysteine rich and form disulfide bridges with chaperone lipids.

24. Identify the following group that contains only amino acids that can form hydrogen bonds with water.
    (A) Serine, tyrosine, glutamine
    (B) Aspartic acid, glutamic acid
    (C) Leucine, alanine, valine
    (D) Ornithine, homocysteine, homoserine
    (E) Arginine, histidine, lysine

25. What characteristic allows laboratory separation of proteins by immuno-electric focusing?
    (A) Overall tyrosine content
    (B) Number of disulfide bridges
    (C) Protein mass
    (D) Number of a-helices
    (E) Isoelectric point

26. One common clinical evaluation for serum protein disorders is serum protein electrophoresis (SPEP). What abnormalities does this technique detect?

    (A) Iron deficiencies in hemoglobin
    (B) C3 or C4 deficiencies
    (C) Clotting irregularities
    (D) Excessive water retention
    (E) Abnormal protein levels

27. Other than the fact that they are both proteins, in what way are enzymes and antibodies similar?

    (A) Both are cysteine rich.
    (B) Both are heavily glycosylated.
    (C) Both rely on induced fit for function.
    (D) Both are primarily hydrophobic.
    (E) Both have a complex quaternary structure.

28. In what way are proteins related to hair perms?

    (A) The treatment permanently denatures hair proteins.
    (B) The treatment reversibly alters disulfide bridges.
    (C) The degree of protein glycosylation is changed by the treatment.
    (D) Hair keratinocyte membrane peripheral proteins are resorted into aggregates that change the hair shape.
    (E) The treatment substitutes tyrosine for phenylalanine residues.

29. Which of the following is true about the peptide bond?

    (A) The bond is planar.
    (B) The bond is formed by a hydrolysis reaction.
    (C) The bond involves the R–side chains.
    (D) The bond is ionic.
    (E) The bond formation is irreversible.

30. What a coenzyme is to increasing enzyme activity, _____ is to decreasing it.

    (A) end product inhibition
    (B) repression
    (C) competitive inhibition
    (D) allosteric inhibition
    (E) steric interference

31. How can you tell if a substance acts as a competitive or a noncompetitive inhibitor?
    (A) Increasing the concentration of a noncompetitive inhibitor will increase the inhibition effect.
    (B) Noncompetitive inhibitors affect only enzymes lacking disulfide bridges.
    (C) Increasing the concentration of a competitive inhibitor will increase the inhibition effect.
    (D) Increasing the concentration of a noncompetitive inhibitor will decrease the inhibition effect.
    (E) Increasing the concentration of a competitive inhibitor will decrease the inhibition effect.

32. The presence of an enzyme such as lysine deaminase can be used in the species identification of some pathogenic bacteria. Into which enzyme class does this enzyme fall?
    (A) Transferase
    (B) Oxidoreductase
    (C) Isomerase
    (D) Ligase
    (E) Lyase

33. When lagging strand synthesis takes place during DNA replication, periodic nicks in the newly synthesized strand that demark the limits of an Okazaki fragment must be repaired to complete the process. Into which enzyme class does this necessary enzyme fall?
    (A) Hydrolase
    (B) Ligase
    (C) Oxidoreductase
    (D) Transferase
    (E) Isomerase

34. The temperature it takes to start breaking apart sucrose is 184°C, yet no known cell can even survive at that temperature, much less also be able to metabolize the sucrose molecule for energy. How can this be?
    (A) Cells use enzymes instead of heat.
    (B) Most cells consume substances other than sucrose.
    (C) Sucrose undergoes spontaneous suicidal degradation at much lower temperatures.
    (D) Most cells can tolerate such high temperatures if they are isolated within very small portions of the cytosol.
    (E) Cells utilize apoptotic pathways to utilize sucrose.

35. Trypsinogen is an inactive protein produced in the human pancreas and then released as part of the pancreatic juice. Upon contact with enteropeptidase in the mucosa of the duodenum, it becomes trypsin. This sequence means that trypsinogen is classified as a

(A) cofactor.
(B) coenzyme.
(C) vitamin.
(D) zymogen.
(E) digest.

36. When a transport protein moves two different substances simultaneously across a membrane in opposite directions, this operation is called

(A) duoport.
(B) symport.
(C) antiport.
(D) uniport.
(E) diaport.

37. Can a protein be used for energy storage?

(A) Yes, but only in the liver.
(B) Yes; proteins store about 4 kcal per gram.
(C) No; energy storage is reserved for carbohydrates.
(D) No; energy storage is reserved for lipids.
(E) Yes, but only in thermophilic bacteria.

38. Proteins are continually being simultaneously manufactured and degraded within any viable cell. However, in an animal that is breaking down more protein than it is synthesizing, what is one problem with which it must deal?

(A) A deficit of free energy
(B) A drop in cellular pH
(C) The buildup of sodium ions
(D) A loss of calcium ions
(E) A surplus of amine groups

39. Leonor Michaelis and Maud Menten are best known for their work in

(A) quantitating enzyme kinetics.
(B) measuring antigen-antibody binding potential.
(C) developing protein sequencing methodologies.
(D) constructing chiral diffraction gratings.
(E) designing the first automated protein synthesizer.

40. At least what assumption must be made in order for the Michaelis-Menten equation to be accurate?
    (A) The enzyme must be continually replaced during the reaction.
    (B) The catalyzed reaction must progress only in the forward direction.
    (C) The enzyme concentration must be much less than the substrate concentration.
    (D) The forward rate of the catalyzed reaction must be equal to the reverse rate.
    (E) The reaction must take place under conditions of standard temperature and pressure.

41. Which of the following must be present in order for a protein-based molecular motor to function properly?
    (A) An elevated pH
    (B) Free ATP
    (C) Magnesium ions
    (D) Inorganic phosphate
    (E) Calcium ions

42. A researcher was looking into the enzyme lactate dehydrogenase (LDH) as isolated from three patients with a certain blood abnormality. When comparing the rate kinetics for the three LDH samples isolated, she discovered that the K_m and V_{max} for all three were uniquely different. This led the researcher to accurately suspect that
    (A) the samples were contaminated.
    (B) each sample required a different coenzyme.
    (C) the condition was sex-linked.
    (D) the rate calculations were invalid for this condition.
    (E) different isoenzymes had been isolated.

CHAPTER 2

Molecular Biology

43. Which of the following elements is NOT required for a cell to synthesize DNA?

(A) Phosphorus
(B) Nitrogen
(C) Hydrogen
(D) Carbon
(E) Iron

44. Which of the following DNA sequences is least likely to represent a restriction endonuclease cut site?

(A) AGCT
(B) GACGAC
(C) GGATCC
(D) AAGCTT
(E) GATATC

45. In genetic engineering, the term "sticky ends" refers to

(A) the effects on mRNA following posttranscriptional modification within the nucleus.
(B) the results on DNA following the work of the DNA replisome.
(C) the product produced by most restriction enzymes.
(D) the physiologic changes produced by an inversion mutation.
(E) the increased production of glycolipids following induction of the glucose operon.

46. DNA ligase is used to

  (A) initiate DNA synthesis in prokaryotes.
  (B) stabilize the DNA helix to prevent supercoiling during DNA replication.
  (C) identify the site on an operon where RNA-polymerase binds to the DNA helix.
  (D) join together Okazaki fragments during lagging-strand DNA synthesis.
  (E) initiate DNA synthesis in eukaryotes.

47. If the base sequence triplet AAC was found on the DNA sense strand, what would be the resulting amino acid added within the ribosome?

Second base in codon

		U	C	A	G	
		Phe	Ser	Tyr	Cys	U
	U	Phe	Ser	Tyr	Cys	C
		Leu	Ser	STOP	STOP	A
		Leu	Ser	STOP	Trp	G
		Leu	Pro	His	Arg	U
	C	Leu	Pro	His	Arg	C
		Leu	Pro	Gln	Arg	A
		Leu	Pro	Gln	Arg	G
First base in codon		Ile	Thr	Asn	Ser	U
	A	Ile	Thr	Asn	Ser	C
		Ile	Thr	Lys	Arg	A
		Met	Thr	Lys	Arg	G
		Val	Ala	Asp	Gly	U
	G	Val	Ala	Asp	Gly	C
		Val	Ala	Glu	Gly	A
		Val	Ala	Glu	Gly	G

Third base in codon

  (A) Leucine
  (B) Asparagine
  (C) Proline
  (D) None; it codes for a halt to protein synthesis
  (E) Glycine

Passage 2: Questions 48–52

While today site-directed mutagenesis has greatly streamlined research in genetic expression, labs that are less well funded or reliant on older techniques can still produce advances within the field, albeit at a much slower pace. One such researcher was utilizing near-visible ultraviolet light as a mutagen in investigating the efficiency of such light sources used in commercial bakeries. This researcher was utilizing *Serratia marcescens*, a coliform bacterium, as the reporter organism because of its intense red pigment when grown under standard conditions.

The technique being used is replica plating, where organisms are irradiated and grown on nutritionally complete agar medium, and then the respective colonies are transferred via sterile cloth-covered plates that reproduce the exact same colony location onto media that are deficient in one or more components. Mutants are detected by their colonial presence on the complete medium but their absence on the deficient medium. The colony present on the original medium is then used as the source for mutant studies. In this case, the lab is studying *lac* operon expression. The researchers used this older technique and observed the following.

48. One colony failed to grow on the replica plate that contained glucose as the sole carbon source. What is the most likely cause?

   (A) A point mutation in the beta-galactosidase gene
   (B) A frame-shift mutation in the genome at a location other than the *lac* operon
   (C) An inversion mutation within the promoter region of the *lac* operon
   (D) A deletion mutation of the lactose repressor gene

49. One colony failed to grow only on the replica plate that contained lactose as the sole carbon source. What is the most likely cause?

   (A) A point mutation in the beta-galactosidase gene
   (B) A frame-shift mutation in the genome at a location other than the *lac* operon
   (C) An inversion mutation within the promoter region of the *lac* operon
   (D) None of the above

50. One colony was discovered to have changed from inducible to constitutive *lac* expression. What is the most likely cause?

   (A) A point mutation in the beta-galactoside permease gene
   (B) A frame-shift mutation in the genome at a location other than the *lac* operon
   (C) An inversion mutation within the operator region of the *lac* operon
   (D) None of the above

51. An extracellular material that was capable of passing through a 0.2-μm filter was found to be able to change pigment expression from pigment negative to pigment positive in species other than *S. marcescens*. The material was possibly

    (A) a phage.
    (B) a DNA fragment.
    (C) a plasmid.
    (D) all of the above.

52. In order to help determine which material in the previous question was responsible for the pigment change, which technique could eliminate one of the possibilities?

    (A) Protein precipitation
    (B) Passage through a poly-T affinity column
    (C) Passage through a poly-A affinity column
    (D) Passage through a 0.1-μm filter

53. Which of the following mutations is most likely to produce a lethal condition?

    (A) A point substitution within the region coding for the leader segment of the mRNA coding for a critical enzyme
    (B) An inversion within a region coding for an intron within the mRNA coding for a critical enzyme
    (C) A point substitution within the TATAAT box within the promoter for the gene coding for a critical enzyme
    (D) A frame-shift mutation within a region coding for an intron within the mRNA coding for a noncritical enzyme
    (E) A silent mutation within a gene coding for a critical enzyme

54. Which of the following enzymes was discovered as a result of research into why bacteria could survive infections with bacteriophages?

    (A) β-lactamase
    (B) DNA ligase
    (C) DNA-dependent RNA-polymerase
    (D) RNA-dependent DNA polymerase
    (E) Restriction endonuclease

55. Bacterial transcription requires the presence of what is known as a sigma (σ-) subunit. Why is this component important?
    (A) It must be present to properly locate the poly-A tail.
    (B) It must be present in order for the RNA-polymerase to properly locate the promoter region.
    (C) It must be present in order to properly ligate the Okazaki fragments.
    (D) It is required to properly terminate the process of transcription.
    (E) It is required as a cofactor of the RNA-polymerase and must be present throughout the process to maintain transcription.

56. DNA-dependent RNA polymerase functions
    (A) only within the nucleus and ribosomes.
    (B) only within the nucleus.
    (C) only within the nucleus, mitochondria, and ribosomes.
    (D) only within the nucleus, mitochondria, and chloroplasts.
    (E) only within the mitochondria and chloroplasts.

57. Where are ribosomes found within a cell?
    (A) Only within the cytoplasm
    (B) Within the cytoplasm and endoplasmic reticulum
    (C) Within the cytoplasm, mitochondria, and chloroplasts
    (D) Only within the nucleus
    (E) Only within the endoplasmic reticulum

58. Which of the following is the best distinction between DNA and RNA?
    (A) Base pairing occurs only in DNA.
    (B) Adenine base pairs with uracil in DNA but with thymidine in RNA.
    (C) The sugar-phosphate-sugar-phosphate repeating backbone structure is found only in DNA.
    (D) The backbone in RNA contains fewer oxygen atoms than that found in DNA.
    (E) Only DNA is found in the eukaryotic nucleus.

59. All of the following enzymes are required for DNA replication EXCEPT
    (A) endonuclease.
    (B) ligase.
    (C) DNA polymerase.
    (D) topoisomerase.
    (E) helicase.

60. Ribosomes are responsible for what cellular activity?

    (A) Translation
    (B) Glycosylation and assembly of proteins
    (C) Polyadenylation
    (D) Reverse transcription
    (E) Posttranscriptional modification

61. A frame-shift mutation within a region coding for an intron

    (A) would result in the cell's death because all genes coded downstream would be affected.
    (B) would result in the cell's death because no RNA-polymerase binding site found downstream would be recognizable.
    (C) would have no real effect on the cell because the frame shift would be corrected during transcription.
    (D) would result in the cell's death because the resulting message could not be translated.
    (E) would have no real effect on the cell because the intron would still be properly spliced out.

62. Which of the following codon pairs would most likely code for the same amino acid because of the wobble in the genetic code?

    (A) AAC and ACC
    (B) UUU and UUA
    (C) UUA and CUA
    (D) GGG and CCC
    (E) CAU and UAC

63. The phases of translation consist of

    (A) initiation and translation.
    (B) initiation, elongation, and termination.
    (C) elongation, continuation, and termination.
    (D) initiation, elongation, modification, and termination.
    (E) initiation and termination.

64. Which of the following sequences would hybridize the strongest to the sequence 5′-ATTTGGGCCAATGGGCCCTTTAA-3′?

    (A) 5′-ATTTGGGCCAATGGGCCCTTTAA-3′
    (B) 3′-ATTTGGGCCAATGGGCCCTTTAA-5′
    (C) 3′-TATTCCCGGTTACCCGGGAAATT-5′
    (D) 5′-TATTCCCGGTTACCCGGGAAATT-3′
    (E) 3′-TAAACCCCCAATCCCGGGAAATT-5′

65. Ultraviolet light is carcinogenic because

(A) it produces thymidine dimers that interfere with DNA replication and cell control.

(B) it causes base pairing mismatches that interfere with DNA replication.

(C) it produces massive amounts of degraded DNA that prevents the replication of exposed cells.

(D) it produces massive amounts of degraded DNA that causes the loss of the ability to control cell growth.

(E) it produces inversion mutations that interfere with cellular control.

66. When comparing the structure of bacterial and eukaryotic DNA, it is observed

(A) that bacterial DNA is thinner and less complex.

(B) that bacterial DNA contains uracil instead of thymidine.

(C) that bacterial and eukaryotic DNA are identical in structure.

(D) that bacterial DNA is interpreted with a different genetic code than eukaryotes.

(E) that bacterial DNA is constructed with ribose rather than deoxyribose.

67. The Shine-Dalgarno sequence is recognized by

(A) a ribosome.

(B) a replisome.

(C) a restriction endonuclease.

(D) a splicesome.

(E) a sigma factor.

68. RNA is believed to be a more primitive molecule than DNA because

(A) it is more flexible in structure.

(B) it uses a less complex base pairing system.

(C) RNA lacks the base pairing system used by DNA.

(D) RNA can have catalytic properties.

(E) RNA is always a much shorter molecule than DNA.

69. Intact ribosomes are assembled

(A) within the nucleolus of the cell.

(B) at the nuclear pores of the cell.

(C) at the location of transcription in eukaryotes.

(D) within the Golgi bodies of eukaryotes.

(E) within the cytoplasm of the cell.

70. Which of the following increases fidelity during replication?

    (A) SOS repair
    (B) Excision repair
    (C) Photoreactivation of thymidine dimers
    (D) Recombination repair
    (E) Exonuclease proofreading

71. If a nucleic acid was found in a cell with a long terminal repetitive sequence of adenines, then it would probably be

    (A) synthetic and inserted by researchers.
    (B) mRNA.
    (C) cDNA.
    (D) a waste product of posttranscriptional modification.
    (E) rDNA, with the repetitive sequence representing the last exon.

72. What enzyme(s) is/are used by researchers to excise genes of interest?

    (A) DNA-dependent RNA polymerase
    (B) DNA-dependent DNA polymerase
    (C) DNA ligase and primase
    (D) Restriction endonucleases
    (E) RNA-dependent RNA polymerase

73. Which base pairing below represents the strongest binding?

    (A) A-T
    (B) C-A
    (C) G-T
    (D) G-C
    (E) A-U

74. The function of which of the following is utilized in lagging-strand synthesis but not leading-strand synthesis?

    (A) DNA ligase
    (B) Helicase
    (C) Topoisomerase
    (D) DNA-dependent DNA polymerase
    (E) Sigma factor

75. The analogous sequence found in eukaryotes to that of the Pribnow box found in prokaryotes is
   (A) TAATAT.
   (B) TATAAT.
   (C) TATA.
   (D) TAAT.
   (E) ATAT.

76. The expression "replication is semiconservative" means that
   (A) DNA replicates in a more effective manner than RNA.
   (B) one original strand base-paired to one newly synthesized strand is the result of replication.
   (C) DNA replicates in a more efficient manner than RNA.
   (D) following replication, one copy is composed of only newly synthesized DNA, while the other contains the original template strands.
   (E) both copies of DNA following replication are almost, but not quite, exact copies of the originals.

77. Which of the following mechanisms of DNA repair are mediated by the *rec*A protein?
   (A) Exonuclease proofreading
   (B) Photoreactivation
   (C) SOS repair
   (D) Excision repair
   (E) Recombination repair

78. What do cellular tRNA, rRNA, and mRNA NOT have in common?
   (A) They are all synthesized within the nucleus in eukaryotes.
   (B) They all contain uracil in lieu of thymine.
   (C) They are all present during translation.
   (D) They all can form short complementary double-stranded regions with each other.
   (E) They all code for the production of some protein product.

79. During PCR, what mechanism is used to separate the complementary DNA strands from each other?
   (A) Heating
   (B) The use of the melting capability of DNA polymerase
   (C) The inclusion of bacterial ribosomes
   (D) The inclusion of restriction endonucleases
   (E) The addition of large amounts of sodium chloride

80. In order to isolate genes for cloning into another organism, DNA is frequently fragmented by enzymes. In order to purify these fragments, what is done next?

(A) The fragments are separated by gradient ultracentrifugation.
(B) The desired fragments are removed from the solution by affinity chromatography.
(C) The various fragments are separated from each other by agarose gel electrophoresis.
(D) The fragments are separated from each other by a series of filtration steps using filters with differing pore sizes.
(E) Specific bacteria are added to the solution because selected species will allow specific sequences of foreign DNA to be incorporated into their own.

81. During translation, how is the subsequent amino acid transferred from the tRNA that brought it into the ribosome to the nascent protein strand?

(A) The two are brought into very close proximity, and the amino acid spontaneously joins the polypeptide due to hydrophobic interactions.
(B) The transfer requires the expense of ATP to break one bond and form the other.
(C) The rRNA of the ribosome serves to catalyze the transfer from the tRNA to the polypeptide strand.
(D) Two proteins of the large ribosomal subunit facilitate the transfer from the tRNA to the polypeptide strand.
(E) The interactions of the proteins and rRNA of both ribosomal subunits physically distort the tRNA–amino acid bond to the breaking point, allowing its facilitated transfer to the polypeptide.

82. Which of the following is responsible for the synthesis of tRNA?

(A) DNA polymerase I
(B) RNA polymerase II
(C) DNA polymerase III
(D) RNase
(E) RNA polymerase III

83. The cumulative length of DNA within a single human nucleus, if laid end to end, would be about 1.8 meters. Of that, approximately how much codes for human proteins?

(A) 14 cm
(B) 50 cm
(C) 3.6 cm
(D) 5.4 cm
(E) 61 cm

CHAPTER 3

Genetics and Evolution

84. What is the best way to express the difference between a genotype and a genome?

(A) Two organisms may vary in genotype as a result of differences in DNA sequences but have the same genome because they have the same genes.

(B) One organism may have one genome but two genotypes if the genotypes are diploid.

(C) Eukaryotes have genomes; prokaryotes have genotypes.

(D) A genotype represents the sequence of gene loci, while a genome represents the sequence of DNA bases.

(E) Eukaryotes have genotypes; prokaryotes have genomes.

85. Which of the following is true about a human male's karyotype?

(A) There are 23 homologous chromosomes.

(B) The banding patterns for all chromosomes in a single nucleus are identical.

(C) The banding patterns for all autosomes in a single nucleus are identical.

(D) All chromosomes are in matching pairs.

(E) There are 22 homologous chromosome pairs.

86. Klinefelter's syndrome is indicated by an XXY sex chromosome combination. This abnormality is due to:

(A) gene deletion.

(B) gene duplication.

(C) nondisjunction.

(D) gene translocation.

(E) infertility.

87. The human ABO blood groups are under _____ inheritance control.
    (A) simple-dominance
    (B) codominance
    (C) partial-dominance
    (D) incomplete-dominance
    (E) epistatic

88. Which of the following is NOT true concerning the process of meiosis?
    (A) Alternate forms of the genes are shuffled.
    (B) Parental DNA is divided and distributed to gametes.
    (C) The diploid number of chromosomes is changed from diploid to haploid.
    (D) Offspring are provided with new gene combinations.
    (E) Meiosis is a process that occurs only in the ovaries but not in the testes.

89. _____ is a genetic disorder in which the individual has a mutation in an ion channel protein.
    (A) Tay-Sachs disease
    (B) Hemophilia
    (C) Sickle cell disease
    (D) Cystic fibrosis
    (E) Phenylketonuria

90. When a mother cell gives rise to four genetically different daughter cells, the process is known as
    (A) a series of mutations.
    (B) meiosis.
    (C) cloning.
    (D) mitosis.
    (E) genetic engineering.

91. A father with type A blood and a mother with type B blood
    (A) will always have children with blood type A.
    (B) will always have children with blood type B.
    (C) will never have children with blood type O.
    (D) will have children with blood type O more often than not.
    (E) will have children of all blood types, depending on the parental genotypes.

92. By convention, a genotype of *RR* would indicate
    (A) homozygous dominant on any chromosome.
    (B) heterozygous on male sex chromosomes.
    (C) homozygous recessive on autosomes.
    (D) heterozygous on autosomes.
    (E) hemizygous on female sex chromosomes.

93. Which is NOT true of human chromosomes?
    (A) The haploid number is 23.
    (B) Somatic cells contain a total of 46 chromosomes.
    (C) There are 23 pairs of chromosomes.
    (D) Gametes contain two of each of 23 chromosomes.
    (E) The diploid number is 46.

94. A mutation is most correctly defined as
    (A) any change in the DNA sequence.
    (B) a detrimental change in phenotype.
    (C) any change from the wild type.
    (D) a change in DNA that has a lethal effect.
    (E) any change except one that has a neutral effect.

95. To express an X-linked recessive trait
    (A) a male must be heterozygous for that trait.
    (B) a female must be homozygous for that trait.
    (C) a male must be homozygous for that trait.
    (D) a female must be heterozygous for that trait.
    (E) a female must be hemizygous for that trait.

96. A person with Tay-Sachs disease
    (A) has a sex-linked condition.
    (B) has a mutation in a gene that controls lipid production.
    (C) suffers from frequent bruising.
    (D) must limit the amount of meat in the diet.
    (E) is incapable of having male children.

97. In genetics, a locus is
    (A) a recessive gene.
    (B) a sex chromosome.
    (C) the location of an allele on a chromosome.
    (D) an unmatched allele on a sex chromosome.
    (E) a gene that produces a product that regulates another gene.

98. If brown hair is dominant over black hair, then animals that are homozygous and animals that are heterozygous for this trait have the same
    (A) genotypes.
    (B) parents.
    (C) phenotypes.
    (D) alleles.
    (E) genetic sequences.

99. Genes that are located on different chromosome pairs
    (A) are sex-linked.
    (B) will appear together in gametes.
    (C) are not able to affect each other's expression.
    (D) will sort independently.
    (E) are identified as being linked.

100. A syndrome is a
    (A) genetic disorder.
    (B) group of signs and symptoms that tend to appear together.
    (C) series of fragile chromosomes.
    (D) disease that is undefined.
    (E) series of conditions that are rarely encountered.

101. Which of the following is true about mitochondrial genetics?
    (A) Human cells contain only maternal mitochondria.
    (B) Mitochondria replicate and function independently of the nucleus.
    (C) Mitochondria have been found in some very large bacteria.
    (D) The mitochondrial genome is invariant in humans.
    (E) Mitochondrial genes more closely resemble eukaryotic than prokaryotic genes.

102. If a person acquired a mutation that was detected in the DNA but that did not change any protein, then which of the following CANNOT be true?
    (A) The mutation was a silent mutation.
    (B) The mutation occurred within an intron.
    (C) The mutation was a neutral mutation.
    (D) The mutation was a deletion mutation.
    (E) The mutation was an inversion mutation.

103. A simple-dominance monohybrid test crossed with a heterozygote will result in a ratio of

(A) 1:3.
(B) 1:2:1.
(C) 1:2:2:1.
(D) 1:1.
(E) 9:3:3:1.

104. If a daughter expresses a recessive gene that has a known simple-dominance sex-linked inheritance pattern, then which of the following is true?

(A) She inherited the trait from her mother only.
(B) All of her sisters would also express that trait.
(C) She inherited the trait from her father only.
(D) All of her brothers and sisters would also express that trait.
(E) She inherited the trait from both parents.

105. Which of the following genetic conditions confers both an affliction and an advantage on an individual?

(A) Color blindness
(B) Blood group AB^+
(C) Turner syndrome
(D) Sickle cell anemia
(E) Down syndrome

106. Identify the result of incomplete dominance.

(A) A man with blood group O
(B) Having medium-thickness hair from a parent with thin hair and a parent with thick hair
(C) A woman with blood group AB
(D) A person with long toes who has parents with short toes
(E) A person lacking hair who has two normal parents

107. What would be the most likely result if a person had a deletion mutation in a gene that codes for a single tRNA?

(A) There would be no phenotypic changes because of wobble.
(B) All proteins would be affected, but would still be effective.
(C) The mutation would not be lethal.
(D) There would most likely be significant changes in all proteins.
(E) The mutation would improve cell functions because it would be more streamlined.

108. An individual with a genotype of AaBBCcDd would produce how many different forms of gametes pertaining to these alleles?

(A) 1
(B) 16
(C) 32
(D) 8
(E) 4

109. A centimorgan is

(A) a method to determine genetic defects.
(B) a measure of gene frequency.
(C) a measure of gene linkage.
(D) a method used to suppress some phenotypes.
(E) a measure gene expression in rare events.

110. Which of the following is the most probable expression of epistasis?

(A) When no male offspring are ever born to parents with a certain phenotype
(B) When offspring with brown hair are afflicted, but those with black hair are healthy
(C) When all female offspring die at birth
(D) When parents with the same blood type have a child with something else
(E) When an organism expresses more cellular receptors than normal

111. Which of the following is the best reference to the Law of Segregation?

(A) All chromosomes separate randomly during meiosis.
(B) Every gamete receives a random number of chromosomes.
(C) Gametes receive only one copy of each gene.
(D) Each gene separates from every other gene during meiosis.
(E) Chromatids migrate to opposite ends of the cell during mitosis.

112. If all males in a family are afflicted with a disorder, but females rarely are, then the inheritance pattern is likely to be

(A) codominance autosomal.
(B) incomplete-dominance X-linked.
(C) simple-dominance recessive.
(D) expression of hypostasis.
(E) X-linked recessive.

Passage 3: Questions 113–117

Ornithologists conducting surveys deep within the western regions of the Amazon River basin happened upon a group of uniquely colored parrots that expressed a near-fluorescent yellow pigment in their display plumage that clearly set them apart from others in their population, whose dominant color was a much deeper red. These brighter birds were much more conspicuous within the foliage in which they dwelt, and the researchers thought that this might bring a great selection pressure to bear against this variation. The researchers followed this special population every other summer for a total of 10 years. The data they collected during this period are presented below.

PERCENTAGE OF TOTAL POPULATION IN STUDY YEAR

Group	Year 0	Year 2	Year 4	Year 6	Year 8	Year 10
Red	98	97	95	94	74	75
Yellow	2	3	5	6	26	25

113. A mutation seems to have arisen within this parrot population. At what point was this mutation most likely to have occurred?
   (A) Between years 6 and 8
   (B) Just before year 6
   (C) Before the study began
   (D) Just before the second year

114. Which is most likely to account for the large change between years 6 and 8?
   (A) A mutation that caused a decrease in the average egg clutch size of the red group
   (B) An increase in the longevity of the red group
   (C) The introduction of a strain of bird flu that increased mortality within the red group
   (D) The invasion of a new predator with a preference for the yellow group

115. What conclusion can be drawn concerning the relationship between animal behavior and plumage pigments?
   (A) The yellow pigment is produced because of a change in food preference of the yellow group.
   (B) The red group spends more time exposed to the sun, indicating a photoreactive pigment change.
   (C) The yellow group has a preference for longer baths, producing cleaner plumage.
   (D) None of the above.

116. The researchers in year 10 observed a preference expressed by females of the yellow group for males with the same color. This preference was indicated by a mating bias of 2%. What conclusion can be drawn from this observation?

    (A) The bias is too small to produce any change in the color distribution.
    (B) The mating preference suggests that the mutation might be recessive.
    (C) The mating bias suggests a postzygotic barrier to reproduction.
    (D) The bias indicates that same-color matings produce larger clutch sizes.

117. The change in population colors strongly suggests that what event is being observed?

    (A) Stabilizing selection
    (B) Allopatric speciation
    (C) Directional selection
    (D) Behavioral isolation

118. What do cells showing trisomy 21 and cancer cells have in common?

    (A) Both are aneuploid.
    (B) Both lead to death.
    (C) Both indicate something that is treatable with gene therapy.
    (D) Cells of both types will be detected and destroyed by T_{CTL} cells.
    (E) Both are representative of every cell in the original body.

119. Transfusion of whole blood from Jim to Bill results in clotting and death for Bill. However, transfusion of whole blood from Bill to Jim produces no crisis. Which is the best possible explanation?

    (A) Jim's blood has a much higher concentration of red blood cells than Bill's, and Bill cannot tolerate the difference.
    (B) Bill has type O blood.
    (C) Jim has type O blood.
    (D) Jim is Rh^+, while Bill is Rh^-.
    (E) Jim has had malaria.

120. If GGHH was crossed with gghh, what would be the most common genotype of the F_2 generation?

    (A) GGhh
    (B) GGHH
    (C) ggHH
    (D) GGHh
    (E) GgHh

121. When determining a karyotype, what chemical is commonly added to the collected cells to better observe the chromosomes?
    (A) Acetone
    (B) Colchicine
    (C) Formaldehyde
    (D) Crystal violet stain
    (E) ATP

122. A phenotypic cure:
    (A) can prevent the disorder from being passed on to offspring.
    (B) can eliminate the defective gene in the parents.
    (C) can correct the defective expression.
    (D) can replace the defective gene in the offspring.
    (E) can suppress the defective gene in a carrier.

123. Suppose that, during ovum formation in the ovary, nondisjunction of the X chromosomes occurred and produced two ova genotypes. If these two were fertilized normally, what are the possible resulting genotypes?
    (A) XXY, X0
    (B) XYY, Y0
    (C) XXY, XYY
    (D) XXY, XX
    (E) XX, YY

124. What cell collection method is best associated with fetal karyotyping?
    (A) Cervical scraping
    (B) Phlebotomy
    (C) Buccal swabbing
    (D) Amniocentesis
    (E) Spinal tap

125. Any difference between the percentage of a population having a defective gene and the percentage of the population expressing that gene
    (A) is called dominance.
    (B) is expressed as epistasis.
    (C) is identified as penetrance.
    (D) is measured by application of the Hardy-Weinberg law.
    (E) is called leakage.

CHAPTER 4

Metabolism

Passage 4: Questions 126–130

A series of experiments was run in order to determine the effects of various gases on the growth processes of plants. Each plant was cultured until fully grown in a soil containing an excellent balance of both macro- and micronutrients, and the soil was laden with adequate mycorrhizae culture. After this maturation growth phase, the plants were sealed in separate gas chambers into which a single gas was introduced to replace the normal atmospheric composition. The plants were then given adequate water provisions and observed compared to controls grown under normal atmospheric conditions.

126. If the experimental plants were grown in an atmosphere of pure $^{14}CO_2$ for two days, then harvested and the plant material carbon dated and compared to plant material from control plants grown in a normal atmosphere, what would the carbon date reveal?

(A) The plants would be carbon dated as the same age.
(B) The experimental plants would be impossible to date.
(C) The experimental plants would date as very, very old compared to the control plants.
(D) The experimental plants would not survive two days in their radioactive atmosphere.

127. If the experimental plants were grown in an atmosphere of pure $^{12}CO_2$ for two days, then harvested and the plant material carbon dated and compared to plant material from control plants grown in a normal atmosphere, what would the carbon date reveal?

(A) The plants would be carbon dated as the same age.
(B) The experimental plants would be impossible to date.
(C) The experimental plants would date as very, very old compared to the control plants.
(D) The experimental plants would not survive two days without the presence of ^{14}C.

128. What would be the effect of growing the experimental plants for one week in an atmosphere of pure nitrogen, an essential element for amino acid and nucleic acid production?

    (A) The plants would grow exceptionally well.
    (B) The plants would grow normally.
    (C) The plants would die.
    (D) The plants would become desiccated and lose turgor.

129. What would be the effect of growing the experimental plants for one week in an atmosphere of pure carbon dioxide?

    (A) The plants would grow exceptionally well.
    (B) The plants would grow normally.
    (C) The plants would die.
    (D) The plants would become desiccated and lose turgor.

130. What would be the effect of providing the experimental plants with a normal gas composition for one week, but at one-tenth the normal atmospheric pressure?

    (A) The plants would grow exceptionally well.
    (B) The plants would grow near normally.
    (C) The plants would die.
    (D) The plants would become desiccated and lose turgor.

131. Which of the following is NOT a product of the TCA cycle?

    (A) CO_2
    (B) ATP
    (C) NADH
    (D) Acetyl-CoA
    (E) $FADH_2$

132. When NADH is converted to NAD, the process is categorized as

    (A) dehydration.
    (B) oxidation.
    (C) catalysis.
    (D) reduction.
    (E) exergonic.

133. Homeostasis, the steady state that is so vital to life, is possible for cells because

(A) the cell cannot convert energy from one form to another.
(B) all cells are autotrophic.
(C) the cell continually takes up energy from the environment.
(D) all cellular reactions are anabolic.
(E) all cellular reactions are exergonic.

134. Energy is important to all forms of life because

(A) all forms of life require a continuous supply of it.
(B) it is required in order to do work.
(C) it is required in order to make specific alterations in the cell.
(D) all of the above.
(E) both A and B only.

135. How many enzymatic steps are involved in converting glucose to pyruvate through the process of glycolysis?

(A) 3
(B) 5
(C) 8
(D) 10
(E) 12

136. Of the following components of the mitochondrial electron transport system, which transfers protons in addition to electrons?

(A) Coenzyme Q
(B) Cytochrome a
(C) Cytochrome c
(D) ATP synthase
(E) Cytochrome c1

137. Which of the following would NOT be used as a final electron acceptor in anaerobic respiration?

(A) Sulfur
(B) Protons
(C) Iron
(D) Nitrogen
(E) Oxygen

138. The respiration process that results in the buildup of organic waste compounds in a cell is known as
    (A) dehydration.
    (B) fermentation.
    (C) reduction.
    (D) anaerobiasis.
    (E) oxidation.

139. If 6.5 g of a protein was fully oxidized, what would be the net energy released for use by a body?
    (A) 36 Calories
    (B) 114 Calories
    (C) 26 Calories
    (D) 58.5 Calories
    (E) 6.5 Calories

140. The origin of CO_2 in the blood is
    (A) the natural equilibrium conversion process from O_2.
    (B) glycolysis and the Krebs cycle in tissue cells.
    (C) the product from acting as the final electron acceptor in oxidative phosphorylation.
    (D) passive diffusion from the atmosphere.
    (E) conversion from bicarbonate in the blood.

141. Bacteria are capable of producing 38 net molecules of ATP from every molecule of glucose that is fully metabolized by oxidative phosphorylation. Which of the following is NOT true about this datum?
    (A) The majority of the ATP molecules are produced within the mitochondria.
    (B) This number is greater than that produced from a molecule of glucose within a human cell.
    (C) This total yield of ATP includes the molecules produced by substrate-level phosphorylation.
    (D) The presence of oxygen is required to produce this total yield of ATP.
    (E) This yield includes ATP expenses required to drive glycolysis forward.

142. Frequently the final compound produced by a metabolic pathway will serve as a down regulator for that pathway. This mechanism is known as
    (A) first-product inhibition.
    (B) coenzyme suppression.
    (C) noncompetitive inhibition.
    (D) feedback inhibition.
    (E) steric hindrance.

143. A chemical reaction that results in negative free energy ($-\Delta G$) is considered to be

(A) catabolic.
(B) anabolic.
(C) exergonic.
(D) endergonic.
(E) both A and C.

144. A(n) _____ bond holds the two strands of DNA within its double helix form and must be overcome for gene expression, protein production, and replication.

(A) polar
(B) nonpolar
(C) hydrogen
(D) ionic
(E) covalent

145. For each electron released by an NADH molecule sent through the mitochondrial electron transport chain, _____ ATP is/are produced.

(A) one
(B) three
(C) two
(D) eleven
(E) four

146. Which of the following lipids, as a whole, has the highest burning (smoking) point?

(A) Saturated fats
(B) Polyunsaturated fats
(C) Vegetable oils
(D) Trans fats
(E) Partially saturated fats

147. Any organism that requires organic compounds such as glucose as its energy source would be categorized as a(n)

(A) heterotroph.
(B) lithotroph.
(C) phototroph.
(D) chemotroph.
(E) autotroph.

148. How many molecules of CO_2 are released from a fully oxidized molecule of glucose?
  (A) 2
  (B) 4
  (C) 6
  (D) 12
  (E) 1

149. A(n) _____ bond is formed when monosaccharides are polymerized.
  (A) glycosidic
  (B) peptide
  (C) exergonic
  (D) endergonic
  (E) hydrogen

150. What Le Chatelier's principle is to chemistry, _____ is to biology.
  (A) the Gram stain
  (B) homeostasis
  (C) muscle contraction
  (D) vision
  (E) natural selection

151. In what way is the enzyme catalase related to the food industry?
  (A) It is used in a cold pasteurization process for milk.
  (B) It is used to prevent crystal formation in ice cream.
  (C) It produces a desirable flavor in cheeses.
  (D) It enhances the color of white bread.
  (E) It is used to preferentially isomerize glucose in candy.

152. The action of ATP synthase is commonly attributed to the mechanism of
  (A) symport.
  (B) ligand-gated channels.
  (C) mechanical-gated channels.
  (D) isomeric inversion.
  (E) chemiosmotic coupling.

153. Glucose and _____ are the most closely related.
  (A) starch
  (B) glycogen
  (C) fructose
  (D) dextrose
  (E) cellulose

154. The relationship between glucose and galactose is
(A) that they are pentoses.
(B) that galactose is a disaccharide containing glucose and fructose.
(C) that they are epimers.
(D) that glucose is a disaccharide containing galactose and ribose.
(E) that galactose is a disaccharide containing two glucose monomers.

155. What is the purpose of an equilibrium constant?
(A) To calculate the initial concentration of the reactants
(B) To determine the specific preequilibrium components
(C) To calculate the rate of a reaction
(D) To determine the composition of any system at equilibrium
(E) To identify the component of free energy

156. What is the relationship between an equilibrium constant for any reaction and the free energy of the reaction?
(A) The natural logarithm of K_{eq} is equal to a negative ΔG divided by RT.
(B) The K_{eq} is equal to a ΔG divided by RT.
(C) The K_{eq} is equal to a negative ΔG multiplied by RT.
(D) The natural logarithm of K_{eq} is equal to a ΔG multiplied by RT.
(E) There is no real relationship, as the two are independent of each other.

157. Which of the following are pentoses?
(A) Glucose and lactose
(B) Ribose and deoxyribose
(C) DNA and RNA
(D) Lactase and lactose
(E) Deoxyribose and deoxyfructose

158. What glycogen is to starch, _____ is to _____.
(A) DNA, RNA
(B) peptidoglycan, chitin
(C) a polysaccharide, a monosaccharide
(D) ADP, ATP
(E) a polypeptide, a glycoprotein

159. What is the relationship of acetyl-CoA to the TCA cycle?
(A) The former is composed of the latter.
(B) The former is a product of the latter.
(C) The former feeds into the latter.
(D) The latter is a product of the former.
(E) The two are unrelated.

160. Which of the following is NOT related to a cyclic process?

(A) TCA
(B) Citric acid
(C) Pyruvate
(D) Krebs
(E) Tricarboxylic acid

161. Which of the following processes is especially associated with fasting?

(A) Gluconeogenesis
(B) Anaerobic respiration
(C) Fermentation
(D) Translation
(E) Chemiosmosis

162. What are the end products of the hydrolysis of ATP?

(A) Water and ADP
(B) Glucose, ADP, and inorganic phosphate
(C) ADP, inorganic phosphate, energy, and ketone bodies
(D) The production of ADP and inorganic phosphate, and the release of energy
(E) The release of energy and water

163. The catabolic intermediate _____ is produced by the enzyme _____.

(A) fructose 1,6-biphosphate, phosphofructokinase
(B) phosphoenolpyruvate, hexokinase
(C) 1,3-bisphoglycerate, triosephosphate isomerase
(D) glucose 6-phosphate, enolase
(E) pyruvate, phosphoglycerate kinase

164. Besides the phosphate group, how can NADH and NADPH be differentiated?

(A) By the different structure of the hydrogen added to each.
(B) The former is formed by enzymes, the latter by abiotic mechanisms.
(C) The formation of the former is exergonic, while the formation of the latter is endergonic.
(D) The former is used in catalytic reactions, the latter in anabolic reactions.
(E) Other than the phosphate group, there is no difference.

165. An organic compound that is a carboxylic acid with a long aliphatic tail describes a

(A) nucleic acid.
(B) fatty acid.
(C) polysaccharide.
(D) peptide.
(E) lipopolysaccharide.

166. An organic compound closely associated with photosynthesis, bioluminescence, and apoptosis would most likely be classified as a

(A) fluorochrome.
(B) cytochrome
(C) pigment.
(D) flavoprotein.
(E) peptidoglycan.

167. Which of the following is NOT a characteristic associated with apoptosis?

(A) Blebbing
(B) Inflammation
(C) DNA fragmentation
(D) Chromatic condensation
(E) Cellular condensation

CHAPTER 5

Eukaryotic Cells

Passage 5: Questions 168–172

Common baker's yeast cells, *Saccharomyces cerevisiae*, were suspended in 5.0 mL of a 1 percent glucose solution in a 15-mL test tube (identified as tube A). A second identical tube was also prepared, but without the cells (tube B), and a third tube in which the cells were initially suspended in distilled water (tube C). After 3 minutes' time, 2.0 mL of a 3 percent hydrogen peroxide solution was added to all three tubes, which were then sealed with a pressure sensor. Pressure data were collected at 30-s intervals for 5 min, at which time the tubes were unsealed and 2.0 mL of a 2N HCl solution was added to all three tubes. The tubes were immediately resealed, and pressure data were again collected for 5 min. The pressure, as measured in kPa, is presented below with tubes A, B, and C in sequence from top to bottom.

First 5 Min									
12.6	19.2	27.3	37.6	48.0	56.1	66.4	76.7	88.0	96.9
0.3	0.4	0.3	0.6	0.5	0.4	0.3	0.5	0.4	0.4
11.0	15.2	22.3	31.8	42.1	52.3	62.4	72.5	79.6	92.8
Second 5 Min									
4.3	4.9	5.2	4.8	4.2	5.0	4.3	4.5	5.0	4.9
0.4	0.6	0.5	0.5	0.3	0.4	0.6	0.3	0.4	0.5
3.6	4.7	4.6	4.5	3.8	4.4	4.5	4.5	4.6	4.4

168. What process is producing the pressure?

    (A) The acid is degrading the cells, releasing CO_2.

    (B) A cellular enzyme is breaking down the hydrogen peroxide and releasing O_2.

    (C) Normal cellular respiration is producing CO_2.

    (D) The acid is breaking down the hydrogen peroxide, releasing both H_2 and O_2 gases.

169. Based on the data, what was the effect of adding the acid to tube A?
    (A) The acid disrupted the cell membranes directly, creating an increase in cell volume.
    (B) The acid degraded the hydrogen peroxide, which, in turn, disrupted the cell membranes and cell walls as a result of the buildup of pressure within the cells.
    (C) The acid denatured the enzyme responsible for the gas production.
    (D) The acid reacted chemically with the gas being produced and removed it from the gas phase within the tube.

170. What was the effect of adding the acid to tube B?
    (A) The acid had no effect on the reactions in tube B.
    (B) The acid degraded the glucose present within the tube.
    (C) The acid caused the release of nitrogen gas.
    (D) The introduction of HCl permitted the cells to produce hydrogen gas from the hydrogen ions.

171. What purpose does tube C serve in this exercise?
    (A) It helps determine the role of glycolysis in the gas production process.
    (B) It is present to demonstrate the effect of acid on distilled water.
    (C) It is present to demonstrate the effect of cellular processes on gas production.
    (D) It is present to help determine any effect that cellular metabolism has on the gas production process.

172. If an enzyme was involved in the gas production process, which might it be?
    (A) Catalase
    (B) Beta-lactamase
    (C) Beta-galactosidase
    (D) Hyaluronidase

173. Which of the following cells have the least ability to repair damage in the surrounding tissue?
    (A) Hepatocytes
    (B) Osteoplasts
    (C) Fibroblasts
    (D) Muscle cells
    (E) Chondrocytes

174. Of the following, which indicates protein movement by vesicular transport?

(A) Moving from the cytosol to the nucleus
(B) Moving from the cytosol to the mitochondria
(C) Moving from the endoplasmic reticulum to the Golgi apparatus
(D) Moving from the nucleus to the cytosol
(E) Moving from the cytosol to peroxisomes

175. The flow of ions across a membrane is best associated with

(A) β barrels.
(B) peripheral membrane proteins.
(C) glycosylated proteins.
(D) active transport.
(E) α helices.

176. Which of the following is truest concerning the cytoskeleton?

(A) Cytoskeletons are found in eukaryotes with cell walls.
(B) Cytoskeletons are found only in eukaryotes.
(C) Cytoskeletons are found in plant cells.
(D) Cytoskeletons are found in multicellular organisms.
(E) Cytoskeletons are found in eukaryotic as well as some prokaryotic cells.

177. Which of the following changes to a membrane would increase its fluidity?

(A) Increase the percentage of shorter-chained phospholipids.
(B) Decrease the percentage of unsaturated fatty acids.
(C) Decrease the percentage of shorter-chained phospholipids.
(D) Change the disaccharides to trisaccharides.
(E) Increase the degree of phosphorylation of the lipids.

178. Which of the following is NOT considered a connective tissue?

(A) Collagenous tissue
(B) Cartilage
(C) Adipose tissue
(D) Blood
(E) Muscle

179. Motions expressed by phospholipids in a bilayer include all of the following
EXCEPT
    (A) lateral diffusion.
    (B) rotation.
    (C) flexion.
    (D) flip-flop.
    (E) inversion.

180. Gated transport involves movement of a substance through pores in a
membrane with specific protein accompaniment. Which of the following
identifies a well-known gated transport of a protein?
    (A) Movement from the cytosol into the nucleus
    (B) Movement from the cytosol into the mitochondria
    (C) Movement from the endoplasmic reticulum to the Golgi apparatus
    (D) Movement from the environment into the cytosol
    (E) Movement from the Golgi apparatus to secretory vesicles

181. Which of the following best describes the protein subunits that make up a
microtubule?
    (A) A dimer of intertwined IF polypeptides
    (B) Overlapping layers of actin and myosin
    (C) G-actin monomers arranged into F-actin polymers
    (D) α- and β-tubulin dimers
    (E) Two heavy chains linked to two light chains by multiple disulfide
    bridges

182. Glucose, against a gradient, can cross a membrane by
    (A) simple diffusion.
    (B) channel-mediated passive transport.
    (C) carrier-mediated passive transport.
    (D) carrier-mediated active transport.
    (E) coupled antiport.

183. The length of the hydrophobic tails of the phospholipids of the membrane
ensure the proper chemical characteristics vital to living cells. These are
most commonly within what range of carbon atom length?
    (A) 8–13
    (B) 18–20
    (C) 15–21
    (D) 19–25
    (E) 26–30

184. Protein import into a chloroplast proceeds in the following sequence.

(A) A signal sequence binds to a receptor → the protein-receptor complex moves laterally → the protein refolds → the signal sequence is removed.

(B) A signal sequence binds to a receptor → the protein refolds → the protein-receptor complex moves laterally → the signal sequence is removed.

(C) A signal sequence binds to a receptor → the signal sequence is removed → the protein-receptor complex moves laterally → the protein refolds.

(D) The signal sequence binds to a receptor → the protein-receptor complex moves laterally → the signal sequence in removed → the protein refolds.

(E) The protein refolds → the signal sequence is removed → the protein binds to a receptor → the protein-receptor complex moves laterally.

185. Ribosomal proteins are synthesized in the _____ for transport to the _____ for subunit assembly.

(A) rough endoplasmic reticulum; cytosol
(B) cytosol; Golgi apparatus
(C) cytosol; nucleus
(D) early endosomes; late endosomes
(E) rough endoplasmic reticulum; smooth endoplasmic reticulum

186. Calcium ions in body fluids are normally _____ than in cells.

(A) 200 times lower
(B) 400 times higher
(C) 5,000 times lower
(D) 10,000 times higher
(E) 250,000 times higher

187. Fetal connective tissue is derived from

(A) the ectoderm germinal layer.
(B) placental cells.
(C) the mesoderm germinal layer.
(D) glial cells.
(E) the endoderm germinal layer.

188. Which of the following is NOT a proper epithelial categorization?
    (A) Stratified squamous
    (B) Simple columnar
    (C) Stratified cuboidal
    (D) Complex columnar
    (E) Exocrine gland

189. Glycosylated proteins embedded within the cell membrane
    (A) decrease membrane permeability.
    (B) serve as anchors for the cytoskeletal framework.
    (C) are most frequently associated with cell signaling.
    (D) almost never have disulfide cross-linking.
    (E) are only synthesized during mitosis.

190. Chaperones are best associated with
    (A) vesicular transport.
    (B) protein folding within the lumen of the endoplasmic reticulum.
    (C) protein folding within the cytosol.
    (D) nuclear transport.
    (E) the signal peptidase removal of signal sequences.

191. Which of the following does NOT describes what cytoskeletal microfila-
    ments are responsible for in the eukaryotic cell?
    (A) Amoeboid movement and cytoplasmic streaming
    (B) Forming the cleavage furrow following cytokinesis
    (C) Maintenance of cell shape
    (D) Acting as contractile fibers in muscle cells
    (E) Formation of the interior structure of flagella and cilia

192. Which line of evidence does NOT support the endosymbiotic theory of
    the origin of the mitochondria?
    (A) Mitochondria have their own genome that resembles that of a
        bacterium.
    (B) Mitochondria carry out their own transcription and translation.
    (C) Mitochondria have a genetic code different from that of most of the
        cells in which they are found.
    (D) Mitochondrial membranes are surrounded by an unusual second
        membrane.
    (E) Mitochondria have different forms for RNA than eukaryotic cells do.

193. Reticular connective tissue is best associated with

(A) the endothelial lining of blood vessels.
(B) the structural framework of soft organs.
(C) tendons.
(D) bone tissue.
(E) the matrix supporting adipocytes.

194. Which of the following is the proper sequence of events for a cell undergoing apoptosis?

(A) Nuclear fragmentation → chromosome condensation → bleb formation → DNA digestion → cytoplasmic fragmentation
(B) Chromosome condensation → nuclear fragmentation → DNA digestion → cytoplasmic fragmentation → bleb formation
(C) DNA digestion → chromosome condensation → nuclear fragmentation → cytoplasmic fragmentation → bleb formation
(D) Cytoplasmic fragmentation → nuclear fragmentation → bleb formation → chromosome condensation → DNA digestion
(E) Bleb formation → cytoplasmic fragmentation → DNA digestion → nuclear fragmentation → chromosome condensation

195. Which of the following does NOT correctly describe the structure or functioning of the eukaryotic nucleus?

(A) The inner membrane is lined with a nuclear lamina that binds to chromosomes.
(B) The outer membrane is continuous with the endoplasmic reticulum.
(C) Materials enter into and exit from the nucleus through pores composed of a single nuclear barrel body protein.
(D) Gated transport of a protein into the nucleus requires that it possess a specific amino acid sequence localization signal.
(E) Proteins passing into or out of the nucleus remain in their folded configuration.

196. What prevents glucose from being transported from an epithelial cell out into the intestinal lumen?

(A) The glucose gradient is contrary to this direction of flow.
(B) The glucose is imported with the sodium-potassium pump.
(C) The glucose is imported with sodium antiport.
(D) The glucose is imported with sodium symport.
(E) Too much ATP expense would be required for the cell to drive this function.

197. What is the primary function of the mitochondria within a cell?

   (A) It generates the bulk of the ATP required for cellular functions.
   (B) It regulates all respiration processes.
   (C) It provides all the tRNA used by the cell in translation.
   (D) It serves to break down and detoxify damaging materials generated within the cell.
   (E) It is the site where glycolysis takes place.

198. A material that is NOT associated with the contents of connective tissue is

   (A) elastic fiber.
   (B) tendon.
   (C) collagen fiber.
   (D) reticular fiber.
   (E) ground substance.

199. There are six traits common to all forms of cancer. Which of the following is NOT one of those common traits?

   (A) Evasion of apoptosis
   (B) Autoproduction of growth signals
   (C) Mutagenesis by chemicals or radiation
   (D) Self-sustained angiogenesis
   (E) Insensitivity to tumor suppression

200. Some cellular organelles are present in numbers that sometimes exceed a thousand per cell. Which of the following meets that description?

   (A) Chloroplast
   (B) Peroxisome
   (C) Endosome
   (D) Mitochondrion
   (E) Golgi apparatus

201. Which of the following is correct concerning the relationship between the rough endoplasmic reticulum (RER) and the smooth endoplasmic reticulum (SER)?

   (A) Protein synthesis occurs within the RER, while protein glycosylation occurs within the SER.
   (B) Ribosomes are concentrated near the RER, while they are lacking in the SER.
   (C) Proteins are moved from the RER to the SER by vesicular transport.
   (D) Membrane-bound proteins are synthesized in the cytosol and become embedded in the membrane in the RER, while proteins for secretion are manufactured within the lumen of the SER.
   (E) Protein synthesis occurs within both RER and SER segments, but signal sequences determine into which area they go.

202. Which of the following is the best description for the function of the nucleolus?

(A) It is the primary site of active mRNA production.
(B) It is strongly associated with ribosomal construction.
(C) It is the source of nuclear ATP production.
(D) It is the area of the greatest concentration of RNAi in the nucleus.
(E) It is the area where DNA synthesis is occurring.

203. One cellular organelle is associated with the destruction of phagocytosed materials. That organelle is

(A) the nucleus.
(B) the peroxisome.
(C) the Golgi apparatus.
(D) the rough endoplasmic reticulum.
(E) the lysosome.

204. Apoptosis is a complex mechanism. Which of the following is NOT involved in this process?

(A) Cytochrome c
(B) A death receptor
(C) Caspase
(D) Apoptosome
(E) Peroxisome

205. Which of the following is the best analogous description of the function of the nucleus?

(A) A library
(B) A highway system
(C) A town council
(D) A police department
(E) The power utilities

206. Certain cell types are found only in specific tissues. In which of the following tissues is an M cell found?

(A) Intestinal tissue
(B) Bone tissue
(C) Cartilagenous tissue
(D) Nervous tissue
(E) Muscle tissue

207. Which of the substances listed below is incapable of movement across a membrane without assistance?

(A) Water
(B) Benzene
(C) Sodium ions
(D) Urea
(E) Oxygen

208. Membrane proteins have a wide variety of functions EXCEPT for

(A) transporting substances.
(B) storing materials.
(C) anchoring structure.
(D) serving as a receptor.
(E) enzymatic activity.

CHAPTER 6

Viruses and Prokaryotes

Passage 6: Questions 209–213

The Gram stain is the most common bacteriologic stain used in the clinical laboratory. It consists of the application of a crystal violet solution to a heat-fixed bacterial smear on a glass slide for 60 seconds. The slide is then rinsed gently in distilled water, and an iodine solution is added for 30 seconds. The slide is again rinsed, and a solution of primarily ethanol is rinsed over the slide for 10–15 seconds. The slide is again rinsed, and a solution of safranin is added for one additional minute. After the slide is rinsed a final time and dried, it is then observed with a microscope at 1000× magnification.

209. What category of cells would appear blue after this process?
(A) Cells with thick cell walls
(B) Cells that contain peptidoglycan in their cell walls
(C) Cells with thin cell walls
(D) Cells that lack a cell wall

210. What would be the effect if someone skipped the second step with the iodine solution?
(A) All bacterial cells would stain blue.
(B) All cells would be colorless.
(C) It would have no effect on the final cell colors.
(D) All bacterial cells would stain red.

211. What would be the effect if someone skipped the third step with the ethanol solution?
(A) All bacterial cells would stain blue.
(B) All cells would be colorless.
(C) It would have no effect on the final cell colors.
(D) All bacterial cells would stain red.

212. What would be the effect if someone skipped the heat fixation process?
    (A) All bacterial cells would stain blue.
    (B) There would be no color, as there would be no cells on the slide.
    (C) It would have no effect on the final cell colors.
    (D) All bacterial cells would stain red.

213. What would be the effect if someone stepped away and permitted the crystal violet stain to remain in contact with the cells for 5 minutes?
    (A) All bacterial cells would stain blue.
    (B) There would be no color, as there would be no cells on the slide.
    (C) It would have no effect on the final cell colors.
    (D) All bacterial cells would stain red.

214. What is the truest relationship between a polyhedral virus and a bacterial coccus?
    (A) Their genomes are similar in structure and differ only as a matter of size.
    (B) The only similarity is the relative overall general shape.
    (C) The cell wall of the bacterium is analogous in function to the coat of the virus.
    (D) The cell membrane of the bacterium is analogous in function to the envelope of the virus.
    (E) Both survive only by acting as a parasite on a host cell.

215. The _____ of the bacterial flagella are embedded into the _____ of the bacterium.
    (A) basal bodies; cell wall
    (B) hooks; cell membrane
    (C) axial filaments; outer glycocalyx
    (D) basal bodies; cell membrane
    (E) hooks; cytosol

216. What chitin is to a fungus, _____ is to a bacterium.
    (A) cellulose
    (B) actin
    (C) peptidoglycan
    (D) lactose
    (E) chromatin

217. Some bacteria can form endospores. Which of the following is the best description of these structures?

(A) They are an asexual form of reproduction analogous to the spores of fungi.

(B) They are the only means of sexual reproduction found in bacteria.

(C) They are a survival mechanism for bacteria that is formed when resources become limited or conditions hostile.

(D) They are formed after conjugation, as observed with some enteric bacteria.

(E) They are a fully functioning and metabolizing reduction of the original bacterium adapted to the harsher conditions that triggered their formation.

218. Eukaryotic cells divide by mitosis. Bacteria divide

(A) by lateral schism.

(B) by binary fission.

(C) by meiosis.

(D) by mitosis, where both daughter cells get one-half of the original contents of the mother cell.

(E) by fragmentation.

219. Double-stranded DNA viruses include

(A) Ebola virus and Lassa virus.

(B) bacteriophage T4 and variola.

(C) rhinovirus and poliovirus.

(D) rotavirus and reovirus.

(E) parvovirus and phage φX174.

220. Similarities between viruses and rickettsia include

(A) both metabolize resources from their host cell.

(B) both undergo schizogony to create forms that are infectious.

(C) both spread from host to host by sexual contact.

(D) both are obligate intracellular parasites.

(E) both can be observed inside the host cell by light microscopy.

221. Which of the following mutations restores a bacterial phenotype similar to the wild type, but without restoring the original genotype?

(A) Reversion mutation

(B) Back mutation

(C) Suppressor mutation

(D) Frame-shift mutation

(E) Conditional mutation

222. If a person is taking a prescription of isoniazid (INH), then you can be fairly sure that that person is being treated for a possible infection with

(A) *Mycobacterium* sp.
(B) *Streptococcus* sp.
(C) Herpes virus.
(D) Human immunodeficiency virus.
(E) *Chlamydia* sp.

223. The term "pBR322" refers to a tool used in the genetic engineering of bacteria and is classified as a

(A) plasmid.
(B) restriction endonuclease.
(C) transposon.
(D) restriction fragment.
(E) bacteriophage.

224. Replica plating refers to a technique used

(A) to assure accuracy by running duplicates during phenotyping of new cultures.
(B) to identify proper host-phage combinations.
(C) for standard water analysis.
(D) for the detection of nutritionally deficient organisms.
(E) for the identification of mobile genetic elements with microarrays.

225. Some bacterial plasmids convey an extra degradative or nitrogen-fixing pathway to a host cell. This type of mobile genetic element is identified as a _____ plasmid.

(A) fertility
(B) col
(C) metabolic
(D) virulence
(E) Hfr

226. What do viroids and multipartite viruses have in common?

(A) They are all negative sense viruses.
(B) They are all enveloped.
(C) Their host cells are prokaryotic.
(D) They are all associated with plants.
(E) They are all helical in morphology.

227. The presence of which gas would be toxic for a facultative anaerobe?
    (A) Water vapor
    (B) Oxygen
    (C) Carbon dioxide
    (D) Nitrogen
    (E) Chlorine

228. Genital warts are caused by a
    (A) virus.
    (B) bacterium.
    (C) fungus.
    (D) protozoan.
    (E) microscopic nematode.

229. If you discovered a mutant bacterium that could utilize DNA as a sole carbon source, you would
    (A) panic because it would probably be 100 percent lethal to humans.
    (B) become greatly concerned because it would probably be pathogenic in humans.
    (C) be unconcerned because most bacteria have this ability.
    (D) become somewhat concerned because it would probably reach equilibrium with the human population.
    (E) be unconcerned because this ability would eventually cause it to consume its own DNA.

230. Which of the following statements is true concerning transformation?
    (A) It is the process that enables mitochondria to remain functional in eukaryotic cells.
    (B) A virus stripped of its capsid could still produce a successful infection of a host cell through this process.
    (C) It is the only mechanism that provides genetic mixing in bacteria.
    (D) Seven genera of bacteria use this process to produce endospores.
    (E) *Trichinella* worms use this process to convert adjacent host cells into nurse cells supporting their survival.

231. If the generation time of *E. coli* is 20 minutes and you started with 10 cells in a growing culture, how many cells would you have at the end of three hours?
    (A) 5,120
    (B) 20
    (C) 1,280
    (D) 12,240
    (E) 10,240

232. Bacterial cultures progress through four phases of growth when retained within a closed system. At which phase would you expect the greatest ratio of dead to living cells?

(A) The lag phase
(B) During both the lag phase and the log phase; it would be impossible to distinguish between the two.
(C) The stationary phase
(D) The logarithmic decline phase
(E) The log phase

233. The staining technique used in a microbiology lab to differentiate the two major types of bacterial cell walls is the

(A) negative stain.
(B) endospore stain.
(C) acid-fast stain.
(D) simple stain.
(E) Gram stain.

234. Bacteria and fungi are alike in that

(A) they both can exist in unicellular form.
(B) their cell walls are composed of the same material.
(C) their genomes are organized in the same fashion.
(D) their ribosomes are of identical construction.
(E) they both are capable of both sexual and asexual reproduction.

235. The proper sequence for the replication of a virus within a host cell is

(A) attachment → uncoating → biosyntheis → penetration → maturation → release.
(B) penetration → uncoating → maturation → biosynthesis → attachment → release.
(C) attachment → penetration → uncoating → biosynthesis → maturation → release.
(D) uncoating → maturation → biosynthesis → release → attachment → penetration.
(E) release → penetration → uncoating → attachment → biosynthesis → maturation.

236. If you put hydrogen peroxide on a loopful of bacteria and bubbles were given off, what would you probably conclude about the organism?

(A) It is probably autotrophic.
(B) It is probably aerobic.
(C) Its natural habitat is aquatic.
(D) It is probably an obligate anaerobe.
(E) The organism has a glycocalyx that reacts with the water.

237. If you suspected that someone was showing signs of inhalation anthrax, what would you do?

(A) Rush the person into isolation to prevent them from spreading the bacterium by coughing.
(B) Rinse their lungs with a disinfectant.
(C) Require immediate bed rest to allow their immune system to fight off the infection.
(D) Administer antibiotics immediately.
(E) Administer a whole blood transfusion to provide antibodies to fight off the infection.

238. A viral genome that can be translated by reading the template strand in both the 5′ to 3′ and the 3′ to 5′ directions indicates

(A) it is a virus with an ambisense genome.
(B) it is a virus with a positive sense genome.
(C) it is any virus that requires reverse transcriptase for replication.
(D) an impossibility, as no genome can be so transcribed.
(E) it is a virus with a negative sense genome.

239. If you isolated an organism that lacked a cell wall but had only 70S ribosomes and a circular double-stranded genome, then you would have a

(A) protozoan.
(B) primitive animal.
(C) eubacterium.
(D) mutant fungus.
(E) slime mold.

240. Of the following, which is NOT descriptive of all viruses?

(A) They are all crystallizable.
(B) They all have a lipid bilayer cell membrane.
(C) They all are incapable of metabolism.
(D) They all demonstrate an eclipse period during replication.
(E) They do not grow or differentiate.

241. If you discovered an infectious agent that lacked both RNA and DNA, what would you suspect?

(A) A laboratory error in analysis
(B) A mutant virus
(C) An organism with a new, previously unidentified form of genomic material
(D) An endospore that was so old that its genome had degraded
(E) A prion

242. Bacterial genetic engineers utilize generalized transduction by

(A) allowing a lysogenic bacteriophage to package specific DNA sequences to carry to another cell.
(B) using naked DNA to be randomly taken up by susceptible bacteria.
(C) utilizing a gene gun to insert specific sequences into a cell.
(D) using restriction endonucleases to break apart desired sequences so that they can pass into the target cell for reassembly within the new host cytoplasm.
(E) allowing a lysogenic bacteriophage to package random DNA sequences to carry to another cell.

243. Which of the following best describes how halogens provide disinfection?

(A) By upsetting the osmotic balance between the inside and outside of the cell
(B) By denaturing most organic materials
(C) By disrupting cell wall synthesis
(D) By increasing the rate of efflux of substances from the cell
(E) By decreasing the pH of the interior of the cell to very acidic conditions

244. An infectious agent presenting with a complex protein structure, often incorporating base plates or tail fibers, best describes

(A) a T-even bacteriophage.
(B) a prion.
(C) a toxogenic bacterium.
(D) a bacterium possessing both flagella and pili.
(E) an organism that utilizes schizogony and a reproduction strategy.

245. Bacteria can frequently acquire antibiotic resistance by horizontal transfer. The most common mechanism of this acquisition is by

(A) transformation by plasmids.
(B) generalized transduction by lysogenic bacteriophages.
(C) bacterial conjugation.
(D) classical exchange of equal-sized genome copies.
(E) endocytosis.

246. Bacteriophages have been used as a form of "antibiotic" in protecting humans from bacterial infections. How is it that these viruses do not cause human disease?

(A) Antibodies in the circulation neutralize the viruses.
(B) T-cells phagocytose the bacteriophages.
(C) Human cells do not have the proper phage receptors.
(D) Macrophages phagocytose and destroy the bacteriophages.
(E) The phages are removed from the circulation by attaching to the infecting bacteria.

247. The type of mobile genetic element that has a great similarity to certain types of viruses is

(A) an intron.
(B) an LTR retrotransposon.
(C) a DNA transposon.
(D) a LINE.
(E) a composite SINE transposon.

248. Which of the following best describes the function of RNA polymerase?

(A) It reads a template DNA strand 5' to 3' and synthesizes a DNA strand 3' to 5'.
(B) It reads a template RNA strand 5' to 3' and synthesizes a DNA strand 3' to 5'.
(C) It reads a messenger RNA strand and synthesizes proteins.
(D) It reads a template DNA strand 5' to 3' and synthesizes an RNA strand 5' to 3'.
(E) It reads a template DNA strand 3' to 5' and synthesizes an RNA strand 5' to 3'.

249. The Shine-Dalgarno sequence is found

(A) in the promotor region of inducible genes.
(B) in the operator region of inducible genes.
(C) in the promotor region of repressible genes.
(D) in the leader sequence of mRNA.
(E) on the edges of introns.

CHAPTER 7

Cell Genome and Reproduction

Passage 7: Questions 250–254

Before Mendel, the mechanism by which progeny inherited traits from their parents was poorly, if at all, understood. However, for roughly 150 years following Mendel, research into cellular division and meiosis broadly advanced the understanding of genetics and the role of alleles in variations of characteristics within a population. More recently, the field of epigenetics has greatly expanded the understanding of gene expression and its role in developmental biology.

For each of the following, identify the most likely mechanism that best explains the specific data presented.

250. The isolation of a naturally occurring single-celled organism with 70S ribosomes but lacking a cell wall.

(A) The organism is an L form.
(B) The organism is most likely a strain of *E. coli*, but growing upon glucose-deficient media.
(C) The organism is a peptidoglycan negative mutant of *Trypanosoma crusei*.
(D) The organism is a species of *Mycoplasma*.

251. A Gram positive obligate anaerobic organism, but which can survive in the presence of molecular oxygen.

(A) The organism is *Giardia lamblia* that possesses the peroxidase gene.
(B) The organism is a common species of *Clostridium*.
(C) The organism is a normal morphological variant of *Pfiesteria piscicida*.
(D) The organism is a mucoidal variation of *Bacillus thuringensis*.

252. A cell that can terminally differentiate into any of a number of final cell forms.
    (A) The cell expresses one of a number of variant-specific surface glyco-proteins in sequence.
    (B) The cell is a pluripotent stem cell.
    (C) The cell has a mutation in one of its sigma factor genes.
    (D) The cell has extensive histone methylation.

253. An organism that can express a significant glycoprotein capsule one day but fails to produce it the next under identical environmental conditions.
    (A) The organism was exposed to significant histone acetylation between the two efforts that changed gene expression.
    (B) The organism experienced a base substitution mutation in the promotor region of the capsule coding operon.
    (C) The organism lost the capsule-encoding plasmid.
    (D) None of the above.

254. A cell that disassembles its own nucleus and subdivides its cytosol and organelles into smaller-sized membrane-bound nonfunctional subunits.
    (A) The cell responded to a cytokine signal from a T_{CTL} cell.
    (B) The cell had a response to a bacterial exotoxin.
    (C) The cell had a mutation with a homeotic gene.
    (D) The cell was exposed to conditions that produce septic shock.

255. If you are observing mitosis during metaphase, which of the following would be the correct sequence of structures if you are scanning from one pole of the cell to the opposite pole?
    (A) Centriole → spindle microtubules → kinetochore → centromere → kinetochore → spindle microtubules → centriole
    (B) Centriole → kinetochore → spindle microtubules → centrosome → spindle microtubules → kinetochore → centriole
    (C) Spindle microtubules → kinetochore → centriole → centromere → centriole kinetochore → spindle microtubules
    (D) Centromere → kinetochore → spindle microtubules → telomere → spindle microtubules → kinetochore → centromere
    (E) Telomere → centriole → spindle microtubules → centromere → kinetochore → centromere → spindle microtubules → centriole → telomere

256. Interference in cell-to-cell signaling can be caused by
(A) closed gated transport.
(B) a defective sodium-potassium pump.
(C) antibody binding to surface proteins.
(D) a defect in a gene that codes for part of the cytoskeleton.
(E) increased cholesterol content of the cell membrane.

257. What is the relationship between a centromere and a kinetochore?
(A) A centromere is associated with cellular division, whereas a kinetochore is not.
(B) A kinetochore attaches to the centromere during mitosis.
(C) Kinetochore proteins are phosphorylated to become centromere subunits.
(D) A kinetochore is associated with cellular division, whereas a centromere is not.
(E) Other than the fact that both are composed of proteins, there is no relationship.

258. Which of the following best describes a telomere?
(A) A single stretch of DNA that codes for all nucleic acid polymerases
(B) Regions of intensely staining proteins dispersed throughout chromosomes associated with active transcription
(C) Dispersed DNA sequences that code for most cytoskeletal proteins associated with intracellular communications
(D) Repetitive sequences that are found on the ends of chromosomes
(E) A protein-based structure found in the cytoplasm associated with controlling cellular division

259. The simplest complete summary for the formation of gametes is
(A) $2n \rightarrow 4n \rightarrow 2n$.
(B) $1n \rightarrow 2n \rightarrow 4n$.
(C) $1n \rightarrow 2n \rightarrow 4n \rightarrow 2n \rightarrow 1n$.
(D) $2n \rightarrow 4n \rightarrow 2n \rightarrow 1n$.
(E) $2n \rightarrow 1n$.

260. Which of the following is required for chromosome movement in mitosis?
(A) Microfibril attachment to the nuclear membrane
(B) Microtubule attachment to spindle poles
(C) Myosin attachment at kinetochores
(D) Molecular motors attached to microtubules
(E) Histone attachment to telomeres

261. In what way are the mechanisms controlling gene expression by protein and steroid hormones similar?

(A) Both bind to specific receptors

(B) Both produce second messengers that eventually produce DNA-binding proteins

(C) Both bind to receptors that eventually produce signal production of RNA polymerase

(D) Both specifically bind to surface receptors

(E) Both have structural similarities that allow the cross-reactivity of receptor binding

262. Which of the following is the best description of a proto-oncogene?

(A) A normal important growth-regulating gene

(B) A gene that codes for a catabolite activator protein

(C) A specific gene sequence that is observed in lower animals but that produces pseudogenes in humans

(D) Any DNA sequence that contains a TFIIB recognition element

(E) Any gene that produces an oncogenic effect

263. Certain genotypes of human papillomavirus (HPV) can cause cancer. This ability exists because

(A) the virus causes cell death by interfering with the p53 protein.

(B) the viral E7 oncogene protein binds to protein Rb, thereby preventing the infected cell from controlling its own growth.

(C) viral replication causes disruptions in DNA repair.

(D) viral replication interferes with the *Wnt* control pathway by causing loss of function.

(E) the viral L1 protein disrupts proper chromosome sorting during mitosis.

264. Many researchers are now identifying five, rather than four, stages of mitosis. What is this new stage called?

(A) Isometaphase

(B) Teloanaphase

(C) Interprophase

(D) Pretelophase

(E) Prometaphase

265. What is the relationship, if any, between oncogenes and apoptosis?

(A) Oncogenes code for apoptosis.
(B) Genes associated with apoptosis are usually mutated oncogenes.
(C) A mutated oncogene often prevents apoptosis.
(D) Oncogenes and genes for apoptosis are classified within the same gene family.
(E) There is no relationship between the two.

266. How is an aster associated with mitosis?

(A) Asters form around both centrosomes.
(B) Microtubules attach to the aster.
(C) Asters attach to telomeres prior to mitosis.
(D) Asters are manufactured by telomerases during the G_1 phase.
(E) Asters manufacture the molecular motors used to move chromosomes during mitosis.

267. Which of the following is the best description of a nucleosome?

(A) A cluster of eight identical proteins wrapped around 292 nucleotide pairs
(B) A compact collection of splicing factors and snRNPs
(C) A collection of proteins that aid in the export of ribosomal subunits out of the nucleus
(D) A cluster of four pairs of proteins supporting 146 nucleotide base pairs with attached linker DNA
(E) The region within the nucleus where tRNA and rRNA are transcribed and ribosomal subunits are assembled

268. The component of the RNA polymerase holoenzyme that determines the specificity of the precise DNA binding site in eukaryotes is

(A) the σ^{70} subunit.
(B) the TFIID complex + σ factor.
(C) RNA polymerase I.
(D) the $\alpha + \beta1 + \beta2$ chains.
(E) the $2\alpha + \beta + \beta'$ chains.

269. A chromosomal region rich in simple-sequence repeated DNA describes which of the following?

(A) Microsatellites and telomeres
(B) Telomeres and centromeres
(C) Histones and nucleosomes
(D) Microsatellites, telomeres, and centromeres
(E) Nucleosomes and centrosomes

270. The eukaryotic equivalent of the bacterial hairpin terminator is

    (A) the mRNA leader sequence.
    (B) the 3′ poly-A tail.
    (C) the 5′ GTP triphosphate cap.
    (D) the 7-methylguanosine cap.
    (E) the stop codon in the genetic code.

271. Which of the following is true concerning pluripotent stem cells?

    (A) These cells can be found in only embryos.
    (B) These cells are commonly associated with cancer development.
    (C) These cells can now be fairly easily produced by mutagenesis.
    (D) These cells can be produced from adult cells by genetic manipulation.
    (E) These cells can be found in adult bone marrow.

272. The replisome is best associated with

    (A) transcription of mRNA.
    (B) translation within the mitochondria.
    (C) replication within the nucleus.
    (D) transcription of tRNA and rRNA.
    (E) transcription of cDNA.

273. A ribozyme is

    (A) the enzyme within the ribosome that terminates translation.
    (B) the enzyme within the spliceosome that rejoins exons.
    (C) any RNA that is capable of cleaving itself.
    (D) the enzyme within the spliceosome that rejoins introns.
    (E) a collection of introns that shuts down the transcription of various genes.

274. It has been calculated that, through a mechanism of the accumulation of random point mutations, it would require more than 200 billion years to generate a new functional gene de novo. What alternative mechanism has been suggested as a viable alternative?

    (A) Inversion mutations
    (B) Gene duplication
    (C) Point insertions
    (D) Intentional genetic manipulation
    (E) Massive mutagenic events

275. What evidence suggests that the random inactivation of the Barr body occurs very early in fetal development?

(A) Turtle shells
(B) Armadillo litters
(C) Human maternal twin frequency
(D) Tortoiseshell cats
(E) Inheritance of X-linked disorders

276. What prevents mammals from regenerating limbs much as some salamanders can regenerate a new leg?

(A) Mammals trade regeneration for faster wound healing.
(B) The mammalian genome is much more complex than a salamander's.
(C) The process of regeneration is unique to salamanders.
(D) Regeneration requires specialized tissues that mammals do not have.
(E) Regeneration is more closely related to the process of budding in yeast than to mammalian processes.

277. Does the nuclear envelope always disassemble during mitosis?

(A) No; in arthropods it actually briefly forms an additional outer envelope.
(B) Yes; no exceptions have been found.
(C) Yes, but in some orders the envelope reforms during anaphase.
(D) Yes, but in some orders the envelope reforms immediately upon entering metaphase.
(E) No; it remains intact in lower eukaryotes.

278. The signal that initiates cell cycling through to the process of mitosis is controlled by

(A) phosphokinases.
(B) cyclins.
(C) DNA-dependent DNA polymerase.
(D) ribulose biphosphate levels.
(E) phosphoprotein levels.

279. The most common process whereby a single cell will divide into two genetically identical daughter cells that will, in turn, differentiate into cells that will follow separate differentiation pathways is called

(A) cellular determination.
(B) selection.
(C) discontinuation.
(D) descent through modification.
(E) transposition.

280. How is it that bone marrow stem cells all have the exact same genome, but mature lymphocytes derived from those stem cells, when released into circulation, are all genetically unique?

(A) Insertion sequences invert gene arrangements.
(B) Alternate splicing of mRNA
(C) Epigenetic control of expression
(D) Random movement of DNA segments by mobile genetic elements
(E) Alternate DNA excision and splicing

281. An inversion mutation within spacer DNA would most likely do what to the resulting phenotype?

(A) It would be lethal.
(B) It would prevent the expression of the nearest downstream gene.
(C) It would have no effect.
(D) It would change a constitutive gene into one that was repressible.
(E) The effects of the mutation would be observable only by radically changing the growth conditions.

282. The proper sequence in chromatin packaging is

(A) nucleosome → heterochromatin → chromatin fiber → chromosome.
(B) nucleosome → chromatin fiber → heterochromatin → chromosome.
(C) chromosome → chromatin fiber → nucleosome → heterochromatin.
(D) heterochromatin → chromosome → nucleosome → chromatin fiber.
(E) chromosome → heterochromatin → nucleosome → chromatin fiber.

283. When producing an antibody, a lymphocyte will transcribe a single message. However, two different proteins may be translated from that single mRNA strand. How does this occur?

(A) The message is polycistronic.
(B) The message can be translated in two different directions to produce two different proteins.
(C) Alternate splicing can account for the different products.
(D) Splicing may retain one or more introns that are then translated into a separate domain of the final protein.
(E) The message is dicistronic.

284. When do mitochondria replicate so that each daughter cell receives a sufficient number to be able to continue to function normally after cytokinesis?

(A) S phase
(B) G_1 phase
(C) G_2 phase
(D) Metaphase
(E) G_0 phase

285. If researchers could find a way to discourage or eliminate cellular senescence and aging, what would be a probable outcome?

(A) An increase in cancers
(B) A decreased expression of telomerase
(C) An increase in cellular metabolism levels
(D) An increase in rates of cellular division
(E) A decrease in DNA replication fidelity

286. In what way is fetal development linked to amoebas?

(A) Amoebas are normal uterine flora that help the development of the fetal immune system.
(B) Amoebas produce the same development signals as a fetus.
(C) The blastocyst stage recapitulates colonies of amoebas.
(D) Cells in migration during cellular differentiation produce amoebal structures.
(E) Both are capable of survival in anaerobic conditions.

287. What role does the protein identified as the product of the p53 gene have in development?

(A) It triggers cellular division.
(B) It regulates the rate of cellular division.
(C) It regulates gene expression.
(D) It is key in the selection of which genes are expressed in which order.
(E) It controls which receptor proteins are expressed.

288. When two same-sized chromosomes are found in a nucleus, one from the mother and one from the father, these are referred to as

(A) sister chromatids.
(B) being in synapsis.
(C) duplicate chromosomes.
(D) homologous chromosomes.
(E) sister chromatin.

289. Which of the following is NOT a difference between meiosis and mitosis?

(A) The enzymes produced during the G_1 phase
(B) The amount of DNA in the resulting cells
(C) The genetic composition of the resulting cells
(D) The number of reduction divisions involved in the process
(E) The action of genetic recombination

290. Which of the following is NOT a terminally differentiated cell?

    (A) A dendritic cell
    (B) A platelet
    (C) A megakaryocyte
    (D) A monocyte
    (E) An NK cell

291. Which of the following is NOT known to initiate apoptosis?

    (A) Cell isolation
    (B) Lack of nutrients
    (C) NK cell contact
    (D) Loss of survival signal
    (E) T_{CTL} contact

CHAPTER 8

Cellular Communications

292. Schwann cells are a major component of the _____ system.

    (A) nervous
    (B) digestive
    (C) excretory
    (D) immune
    (E) musculoskeletal

293. The primary neurotransmitter involved at the neuromuscular synapse is

    (A) dopamine.
    (B) histamine.
    (C) D-serine.
    (D) acetylcholine.
    (E) serotonin.

294. The action potential of a nerve cell is maintained by the vigorous activity of

    (A) contractile vesicles.
    (B) sodium-potassium pumps.
    (C) actin-myosin interaction.
    (D) the nodes of Ranvier.
    (E) Ca^{2+} influx.

295. The nucleus of a neuron resides in

    (A) the axon.
    (B) the myelin sheath.
    (C) the cell body.
    (D) a dendrite.
    (E) a node of Ranvier.

296. A nerve is

    (A) a cell of the central nervous system.
    (B) a bundle of neurons.
    (C) a cluster of neurons and nurse cells.
    (D) composed of an axon and numerous dendrites.
    (E) totally surrounded by a myelin sheath.

297. What is the function of an axon?

    (A) It provides for genetic control by being interspersed between introns.
    (B) It provides a physical barrier between the brain and the peripheral nervous system.
    (C) It separates one neuron from another.
    (D) It conducts action potentials from the neuron body to the synapses.
    (E) It establishes the threshold for producing an action potential.

298. The function of the nodes of Ranvier is to

    (A) increase the rate of conduction down the axon.
    (B) increase the respiration rate for higher ATP production.
    (C) decrease the likelihood of "cross-talk" between neurons.
    (D) increase the connectivity between neurons.
    (E) decrease the stimulation required to initiate an action potential.

299. During the transmission of an action potential down a neuron, what is occurring during the depolarization phase?

    (A) Sodium expulsion from the cell drops the polarity to –70 mV.
    (B) The potassium channels open and K^+ diffuses out of the cell.
    (C) The sodium-potassium pumps raise the polarity to +30 mV.
    (D) Sodium rapidly enters the cell, dropping the polarity to +30 mV.
    (E) The sodium-potassium pumps cease working for about 10 milliseconds, and then the voltage stabilizes.

300. What neurotransmitter combination is found only in the brain?

    (A) Acetylcholine and endorphins
    (B) Endorphins and norepinephrine
    (C) Serotonin and GABA
    (D) Acetylcholine and norepinephrine
    (E) GABA and acetylcholine

301. An action potential is propagated down a neuron by

(A) ligand-gated ion channels.
(B) mechanically gated ion channels.
(C) voltage-gated ion channels.
(D) stress-activated ion channels.
(E) unregulated ion channels.

302. Nerve agents such as VX and sarin impair signal transduction through the neuromuscular synapse by

(A) preventing the release of acetylcholine, preventing muscle contraction.
(B) chelating Ca^{2+} ions, preventing muscle contraction.
(C) preventing the reuptake of degraded acetylcholine components by the neuron, greatly weakening muscle contraction.
(D) binding to cholinesterase, preventing the recycling of the neurotransmitter and greatly weakening muscle contraction.
(E) blocking the acetylcholine receptors on the muscle cells, preventing muscle contraction.

303. What cells produce the "white" in the white matter of the CNS?

(A) Schwann cells
(B) Oligodendrocytes
(C) M cells
(D) Macrophages
(E) Dendritic cells

304. What differentiates a stimulatory neuron from an inhibitory neuron?

(A) A stimulatory neuron activates Na^+ channels on the postsynaptic cell, while an inhibitory neuron opens Cl^- channels.
(B) Stimulatory neurons connect to adjacent neurons along the axon, while inhibitory neurons connect to the cell body.
(C) A stimulatory neuron opens Ca^{2+} channels on the postsynaptic cell, while an inhibitory neuron opens Na^+ channels.
(D) An inhibitory neuron releases dopamine, while a stimulatory neuron releases GABA.
(E) A stimulatory neuron passes its action potential through axon bulbs, while an inhibitory neuron conveys it via its dendrites.

305. Certain cell types are found only in specific tissues. In which of the following tissues is a glial cell found?

(A) Muscle tissue
(B) Endocrine tissue
(C) Lung tissue
(D) Nervous tissue
(E) Otic tissue

306. Which of the following is associated with both the nervous system and the endocrine system?

(A) The vagus nerve
(B) Peyer's patches
(C) The vena cava
(D) The hypothalamus
(E) Dura mater

307. The nerves contained within the vertebrae are categorized as part of the

(A) parasympathetic nervous system.
(B) central nervous system.
(C) peripheral nervous system.
(D) sympathetic nervous system.
(E) sensory nervous system.

308. What are the three primary functions of the myelin sheath?

(A) It protects the neuron from infection, it provides some insulation properties for the neuron, and it assists in neuron regeneration.
(B) It provides some insulation properties for the neuron, it serves to increase the speed of signal propagation, and it assists in the formation of synapses.
(C) It assists in neuron regeneration, it provides insulation for the axon, and it serves to increase the speed of signal propagation.
(D) It reduces the neuron's sensitivity to stimulation, it protects the neuron from infection, and it assists in neuron regeneration.
(E) It increases the neuron's sensitivity to stimulation, it assists in the formation of synapses, and it serves to increase the speed of signal propagation.

309. The bulk of the ion channels responsible for action potential propagation are

(A) located along the axon at the nodes of Ranvier.
(B) present at the axon bulbs.
(C) present within the synapses.
(D) located along the axon between the nodes of Ranvier.
(E) at the tips of the dendrites.

310. The parathyroid glands are responsible for
    (A) providing hormones that increase the inflammatory response.
    (B) the production of epinephrine.
    (C) raising calcium levels in the blood.
    (D) regulating diurnal rhythms.
    (E) the production of aldosterone.

311. Type I diabetes is caused by
    (A) the failure of the pancreas to secrete glucagon.
    (B) the presence of excessive adipose tissue that ties up the available insulin.
    (C) the failure of the kidneys to move glucose from the blood to the urine.
    (D) a loss of sensitivity to insulin by somatic cells.
    (E) the inability of the pancreas to secrete insulin.

312. The secretion of ACTH is in response to
    (A) an increased level of epinephrine.
    (B) TSH release from the anterior pituitary.
    (C) increased blood glucose levels.
    (D) long-term decreases in metabolic efforts.
    (E) a release of hormones from the anterior pituitary.

313. At a specific point along a neuron that is propagating an action potential, the sequence of action is
    (A) a flood of potassium into the cell → the action of the sodium-potassium pumps → potassium moves into the cell.
    (B) a flood of sodium into the cell → the action of the sodium-potassium pumps → potassium moves out of the cell.
    (C) the action of the sodium-potassium pumps → a flood of sodium into the cell → potassium moves into the cell.
    (D) a flood of sodium into the cell → potassium moves out of the cell → the action of the sodium-potassium pumps.
    (E) a flood of potassium out of the cell → sodium moves into the cell → the action of the sodium-potassium pumps.

314. The brain has only about 2 percent of the total body mass but consumes about 25 percent of the available glucose. Why is this?

    (A) While it is only 2 percent by mass, the brain actually contains many more cells than the rest of the body combined.

    (B) The brain, because of its control function, is relatively inefficient when compared to muscle cells.

    (C) All neurons must generate huge amounts of energy to maintain membrane polarity.

    (D) Neurons are the primary cell type to maintain proper blood glucose levels.

    (E) Neurons convert glucose to glycogen for energy storage.

315. Which of the following is best associated with the regulation of metabolism?

    (A) Thyroid

    (B) Kidneys

    (C) Liver

    (D) Thymus

    (E) Adenoids

316. The "fight-or-flight" response arises from the release of what hormone(s)?

    (A) Thyroxin

    (B) ACTH and thyroxin

    (C) LH and TSH

    (D) Epinephrine and norepinephrine

    (E) Calcitonin and ACTH

317. A hormone may produce changes within a cell by two mechanisms. One of these is

    (A) binding to surface antibodies attached to mast cells.

    (B) producing cAMP as a second messenger.

    (C) neutralizing the effect of calcium influx.

    (D) increasing neurotransmitter release.

    (E) increasing the strength of muscle cell contraction.

318. The proper sequence of the layers of the meninges, from the outside in, is

    (A) dura mater, arachnoid, pia mater.

    (B) ventricle, dura mater, pia mater.

    (C) sulcus, ventricle, pia mater.

    (D) pia mater, ventricle, sulcus.

    (E) arachnoid, sulcus, dura mater.

319. The portions of the spinal cord that stimulate digestion are the _____ nerves.

(A) cervical
(B) sacral
(C) occipital
(D) cranial
(E) lumbar

320. The posterior pituitary is responsible for the secretion of which hormones?

(A) Glucocorticoids
(B) Aldosterone and epinephrine
(C) FSH and LH
(D) Thyroxine and calcitonin
(E) Oxytocin and ADH

321. The regulation of water concentration in the blood is accomplished by

(A) melatonin.
(B) aldosterone.
(C) testosterone.
(D) HGH.
(E) glucagon.

322. Iodine is an essential element because it is associated with what function?

(A) Control of metabolism
(B) End plate formation in bone growth
(C) Balancing the autonomic nervous system
(D) Control of membrane permeability
(E) Balancing sugar levels in the blood

323. The function of the choroid plexus in the brain is

(A) to serve as a connection between hemispheres.
(B) the production of CSF.
(C) immune surveillance of brain tissue.
(D) generation of the white matter.
(E) to serve as a conduit for CSF flow to the subarachnoid space.

324. Gamma-aminobutyric acid is

(A) a regulator of HGH production.
(B) an enzyme inhibitor associated with HCl production in the stomach.
(C) a neurotransmitter with a role in pain perception.
(D) an animal hormone that has great structural similarities to plant hormones.
(E) a substance that stimulates the production of calcitonin.

325. The master gland of the endocrine system is the

(A) thyroid.
(B) posterior pituitary.
(C) adrenals.
(D) hypothalamus.
(E) anterior pituitary.

326. The portions of the spinal cord that inhibit digestion are the _____ nerves.

(A) thoracic
(B) lumbar
(C) cranial
(D) cervical
(E) temporal

327. Steroid hormones control cell action by

(A) binding to a general hormone receptor on the cell surface.
(B) producing a second messenger after binding to a specific surface receptor.
(C) binding to a nuclear hormone receptor.
(D) passing through the cell membrane and increasing the rate of translation of selected proteins.
(E) increasing membrane permeability for protein transport.

328. The forebrain consists of all of the following EXCEPT the

(A) cerebrum.
(B) pons.
(C) thalamus.
(D) limbic system.
(E) hypothalamus.

329. The mechanism of rapid eye movement is best associated with

(A) the fight-or-flight response.
(B) a sudden release of ACTH.
(C) crossing a threshold for neuron stimulation.
(D) excessive levels of iodine.
(E) the sleep-wake cycle.

330. Which of the following is NOT an effect of long-term stress?
- (A) Organ exhaustion
- (B) Ion imbalances
- (C) Energy depletion
- (D) Adrenal exhaustion
- (E) Iodine insensitivity

331. Which of the following is a CNS depressant?
- (A) Marijuana
- (B) PCP
- (C) Nicotine
- (D) Anabolic steroids
- (E) Alcohol

332. An infant suckling on its mother's breast causes the release of _____ in the mother.
- (A) ACTH
- (B) Bilirubin
- (C) HGH
- (D) Oxytocin
- (E) LH

CHAPTER 9

Internal Movement and Defense

Passage 8: Questions 333–337

Four friends who lived in different states gathered annually for a weeklong elk-hunting trip in Montana for more than 20 years. As part of their tradition, they shared a meal of one of the harvested elk. One of the four was killed in a one-vehicle automobile accident a year ago when he apparently experienced a sudden seizure at highway speeds. Autopsy concluded that the cause of death was due to trauma, but also revealed pronounced spongiform encephalopathy and the presence of significant amyloid plaques in the brain tissue.

Most recently the remaining three have developed similar patterns of memory loss, pronounced personality changes, problems with their ability to balance themselves, and some speech difficulties, and two of them have experienced seizures and depression. This latter issue was initially attributed to the loss of their close friend, but it now appears to be something quite different, but still related to something they all acquired on at least one of their hunting trips. Their physicians are beginning to suspect that the root cause is variant Creutzfeldt-Jacob disease (vCJD).

333. Which is the most likely common source of their combined health issues?

(A) Bacteria
(B) Nematodes
(C) Chemicals
(D) Something other than the above

334. Why would these symptoms be attributed to something acquired rather than to something inherited?

(A) The chances of all four having inherited CJD are very unlikely.
(B) There are very similar diseases caused by encephalitis viruses.
(C) Elk are known to be carriers of an unusual systemic fungus that causes meningitis.
(D) These are characteristics of amoebic meningoencephalitis, probably from the cabin water.

335. What biochemical mechanism contributes to the amyloid plaques?

(A) A malfunction of protein synthesis in the cytosol of neurons
(B) A progressive accumulation of abnormal PrP protein
(C) An error in the posttranscriptional modification of PrP mRNA
(D) Toxin damage to neural synapses

336. How can the agent that causes spongiform encephalopathy remain infectious even after being autoclaved for an hour?

(A) Encephalitis viruses are notoriously resistant to heat damage.
(B) Parasitic amoebas can survive unfavorable conditions in the cyst stage.
(C) The agent is infectious because it is already denatured.
(D) Once melted, DNA is resistant to further heat damage.

337. What process is used to propagate the agent within neurons?

(A) Normal translation of PrP mRNA
(B) Abnormal PrP induces similar abnormalities in normal PrP.
(C) Neurotransmitters act as gene repressors of proteins.
(D) Viral replication in neuron nuclei

338. Following a break in the skin, which of the following is the proper sequence of events that leads to its repair?

(A) Debris removal → clot formation → fibroblast proliferation → inflammation → regeneration
(B) Inflammation → clot formation → regeneration → fibroblast proliferation → debris removal
(C) Clot formation → fibroblast proliferation → debris removal → inflammation → regeneration
(D) Clot formation → inflammation → fibroblast proliferation → debris removal → regeneration
(E) Clot formation → debris removal → inflammation → fibroblast proliferation → regeneration

339. Which of the following are best associated with thermoregulation?

(A) Arrector pili
(B) Sebaceous glands
(C) Apocrine glands
(D) Fingernails and toenails
(E) Meissner's corpuscles

340. Which of the following pairs is NOT correctly associated?

(A) Merkel's disks—sense of touch
(B) Meissner's corpuscles—senses movement of hair shaft
(C) Free nerve endings—sense of temperature
(D) Pacinian corpuscles—sense of pressure
(E) Free nerve endings—sense of pain

341. Fingernail and toenail growth occurs because of

(A) protein synthesis in the nail bed.
(B) osteoclasts laying down nail matrix in the lunula.
(C) epithelial cell division.
(D) synthesis of hardened sebum.
(E) polysaccharide synthesis and export by epithelial cells.

342. Which of the following is true concerning the role of the dermis in nutrition?

(A) The skin helps synthesize molecules that are later activated in the liver and aid in calcium absorption in the intestine.
(B) Cells within the skin manufacture growth factors that provide for improved connective tissue elasticity throughout the body.
(C) It is within the dermis that significant energy is stored in the form of collagenous proteins.
(D) Significant levels of essential minerals are absorbed into the dermis after passing through the epidermis.
(E) The capillary beds within the dermis provide for additional levels of gas exchange with the atmosphere.

343. Of the following, which is the smallest and simplest of the immune components?

(A) Lymph node
(B) Thymus
(C) Lymph follicle
(D) Lymph nodule
(E) Spleen

344. The best definition of a venule is a

(A) vessel of the circulatory system that lacks muscle tissue and conducts blood away from the heart.
(B) vessel of the circulatory system between an artery and a capillary in size that conducts lymph toward the heart.
(C) vessel of the lymph system that conducts lymph toward the heart.
(D) vessel of the circulatory system between a vein and a capillary in size that conducts blood toward the heart.
(E) vessel of the lymph system that conducts lymph from the heart.

345. The cell type that carries the greatest responsibility for phagocytic protection of the body is the

(A) lymphocyte.
(B) neutrophil.
(C) macrophage.
(D) eosinophil.
(E) erythrocyte.

346. Which of the following best distinguishes serum from plasma?

(A) Serum has a higher concentration of proteins than plasma.
(B) Plasma contains a higher percentage of erythrocytes than serum.
(C) Plasma is the same thing as whole blood, while serum lacks the cellular components.
(D) Where plasma contains antibodies, serum contains only the α- and β-globulins.
(E) Serum is the same thing as plasma, but lacks clotting proteins.

347. Which of the following is NOT descriptive of immunoglobulins?

(A) They are composed of three α-chains and one β-chain.
(B) They are glycoproteins found in the blood.
(C) They are produced in large quantities by plasma cells.
(D) They are glycoproteins found in lymph.
(E) They neutralize toxins by binding to complementary regions.

348. The primary lymphoid organs include

(A) the thymus and bone marrow.
(B) lymph nodes and nodules.
(C) the spleen and thymus.
(D) lymph nodes, follicles, and nodules.
(E) bone marrow and the thyroid.

349. The proper sequence in which blood flows through the heart, starting at the vena cava, is

(A) right atrium, left atrium, right ventricle, left ventricle.
(B) left atrium, left ventricle, right ventricle, right atrium.
(C) left ventricle, left atrium, right ventricle, right atrium.
(D) right atrium, right ventricle, left atrium, left ventricle.
(E) left atrium, right atrium, left ventricle, right ventricle.

350. The oxygen level is highest in

(A) the pulmonary arteries.

(B) capillaries.

(C) the pulmonary veins.

(D) the vena cava.

(E) arterioles.

351. Elimination of cancer cells is the responsibility of

(A) T-helper cells.

(B) macrophages.

(C) T_{CTL} cells.

(D) antibodies.

(E) complement.

352. Which of the following is NOT a primary function of the lymph system?

(A) Maintaining proper fluid balance

(B) Production of antibodies

(C) Transport of large triglycerides

(D) Movement of materials from the tissues to the blood

(E) Transport of proteins

353. The proper sequence of actions that bring phagocytic cells from circulation in the blood into infected tissues is

(A) tight binding, rolling adhesion, diapedesis, migration.

(B) diapedesis, rolling adhesion, migration, tight binding.

(C) migration, rolling adhesion, diapedesis, tight binding.

(D) tight binding, diapedesis, migration, rolling adhesion.

(E) rolling adhesion, tight binding, diapedesis, migration.

354. Erythrocytes are best described as

(A) leukocytes that carry oxygen.

(B) thrombocytes that contain iron.

(C) bone marrow–derived cells that carry nutrients.

(D) lymphocytelike cells that carry CO_2.

(E) degenerate cells that contain hemoglobin.

355. After antigenic stimulation, a specific B-cell

(A) will undergo lymphoproliferation, then differentiation.

(B) will start to produce membrane-bound antibodies.

(C) will differentiate into a plasma cell.

(D) will start the manufacture of antibodies for secretion.

(E) will differentiate into a memory cell.

356. The proper sequence for the layers of heart tissue from the outside in is

(A) pericardium, epicardium, myocardium, endocardium.
(B) epicardium, endocardium, pericardium, myocardium.
(C) myocardium, pericardium, epicardium, endocardium.
(D) endocardium, pericardium, myocardium, epicardium.
(E) myocardium, epicardium, endocardium, pericardium.

357. The proper sequence of valves through which blood flows in the heart, starting at the vena cava, is

(A) bicuspid, pulmonary semilunar, tricuspid, aortic semilunar.
(B) pulmonary semilunar, tricuspid, aortic semilunar, bicuspid.
(C) tricuspid, aortic semilunar, pulmonary semilunar, bicuspid.
(D) tricuspid, pulmonary semilunar, bicuspid, aortic semilunar.
(E) tricuspid, bicuspid, pulmonary semilunar, aortic semilunar.

358. What substance dilates blood vessels, increases tissue pressure, and can induce hypovolemic shock?

(A) SRS-A
(B) γ-interferon
(C) IL-2
(D) CD4
(E) Histamine

359. When blood pressure is monitored, two values are determined. What is occurring within the heart during diastole?

(A) The valves are all snapping shut.
(B) Both atria and both ventricles are relaxing.
(C) All valves are open.
(D) The left atrium and the left ventricle are relaxing while the right atrium and the right ventricle are contracting.
(E) The left atrium and the left ventricle are contracting while the right atrium and the right ventricle are relaxing.

360. Which of the following pairs are most closely related?

(A) Monocyte—lymphocyte
(B) Erythrocyte—leukocyte
(C) Macrophage—monocyte
(D) Eosinophil—basophil
(E) Thrombocyte—granulocyte

361. A genetic blood disorder in which regularly shaped biconcave erythrocytes fold under conditions of low blood oxygenation is

(A) sickle cell anemia.
(B) pernicious anemia.
(C) spherocytosis.
(D) hemophilia.
(E) leukemia.

362. Of the following, which is NOT an autoimmune disorder?

(A) Type I diabetes
(B) Rheumatoid arthritis
(C) Hemolytic anemia
(D) Pernicious anemia
(E) Type II diabetes

363. Which chemical would interfere with the purpose of platelets?

(A) SRS-A
(B) Histamine
(C) Heparin
(D) Plasminogen
(E) Serotonin

364. Hematopoiesis is a process that occurs in

(A) the spleen.
(B) the thymus.
(C) lymph nodes.
(D) bone marrow.
(E) areas of infection.

365. The specificity of an antibody is determined by

(A) random gene rearrangements within B-cell progenitors.
(B) antigenic selection of B-cell clones within the bone marrow.
(C) clonal selection by macrophages within the bone marrow.
(D) B-cell response within lymph nodes.
(E) B-cell encounters with foreign antigens.

366. The lymph system connects to the circulatory system

(A) within the spleen.
(B) in lymph nodes.
(C) at the vena cava.
(D) at the capillaries in various somatic tissues.
(E) within the lungs.

367. Which of the following is NOT considered part of the cardiac conduction system?

(A) SA node
(B) M cells
(C) Purkinje fibers
(D) AV bundle
(E) AV node

368. Oxygen and nutrients reach the myocardium

(A) by diffusion through the endocardium.
(B) through two coronary arteries.
(C) by diffusion through the pericardium.
(D) from the pericardial cavity.
(E) through vessels connected to the vena cava.

369. Which of the following antibody classes provides the best protection against microbial invasion through the intestinal mucosa?

(A) IgM
(B) IgD
(C) IgG
(D) IgE
(E) IgA

370. Which of the following is NOT considered a risk factor for hypertension?

(A) Obesity
(B) Smoking
(C) Advanced age
(D) Elevated HDL levels
(E) Elevated sodium levels

371. Which of the following least distinguishes the primary immune response from the secondary immune response?

(A) A difference in time when a maximum response is presented
(B) Which antibody class is predominant
(C) Which antigen is used to stimulate the responses
(D) The level of the antibody response
(E) The role of memory cells in generating the response

372. A differential stain is run by diagnosticians to count the various leukocytes within the blood. Which of the following should always be at the highest level in a healthy person?

(A) Monocytes
(B) Lymphocytes
(C) Eosinophils
(D) Basophils
(E) Neutrophils

373. Which is the proper sequence of events that produces a blood clot?

(A) Calcium binds prothrombin activator → prothrombin activator produces thrombin → thrombin produces fibrin → fibrin produces clot.
(B) Prothrombin activator produces thrombin → calcium binds prothrombin activator → thrombin produces fibrin → fibrin produces clot.
(C) Thrombin produces fibrin → fibrin produces prothrombin activator → prothrombin activator produces clot.
(D) Fibrin produces thrombin → thrombin produces prothrombin → prothrombin produces prothrombin activator → prothrombin activator plus calcium produces clot.
(E) Thrombin produces fibrin → fibrin produces prothrombin → prothrombin produces prothrombin activator → prothrombin activator plus calcium produces clot.

CHAPTER 10

Interactions with the Environment

Passage 9: Questions 374–378

Wood lice were confined within two adjacent corrals (identified as A and B), and were allowed free movement between the two. A total of 10 animals were selected from a group of more than 120, divided randomly into two groups, and then placed into the study corrals five per side. The position of each animal was then recorded at the end of each 60-second period for 10 minutes.

Three exercises were run. The first involved identical environmental conditions in both corrals for 5 minutes, followed by covering corral B with a light shield producing dark conditions for the last 5 minutes. The second involved introducing a moist pad covering the floor surface in corral A while corral B remained dry. The animals were introduced in the same manner and allowed free range, with identical lighting on both sides for 5 minutes followed by a period of darkness only in corral B. The third run differed from the second in that moist pads were present on both sides, but after the first 5 minutes, a mild acid was added to the pad in corral B just prior to the placement of the light shield.

The data collected during these three runs follows, with corral A on top and corral B on the bottom for the three consecutive runs. The numbers in each cell represent the number of wood lice in each corral.

First Run									
4	5	4	7	6	5	3	2	1	3
6	5	6	3	4	5	7	8	9	7
Second Run									
6	7	9	8	7	5	4	5	6	4
4	3	1	2	3	5	6	5	4	6
Third Run									
5	6	6	5	4	6	6	7	4	5
5	4	4	5	6	4	4	3	6	5

374. What combination serves as the best environmental control?

(A) The first half of the first run
(B) Both halves of the second run
(C) The totality of the third run
(D) The totality of the second run

375. What conclusion can be drawn concerning the animals' preference for a moist environment?

(A) The animals have no preference.
(B) The animals prefer a dry environment regardless of other conditions.
(C) The animals prefer a moist environment, but only in the dark.
(D) The animals prefer a moist environment when under lighted conditions.

376. What conclusion can be drawn concerning the animals' preference for an acid environment?

(A) The animals clearly prefer a nonacid environment.
(B) There is no evidence to support a conclusion either way.
(C) The animals appear to prefer an acid environment.
(D) An acid environment is preferred, but only in the dark.

377. What conclusion can be drawn concerning the animals' preference for light versus dark conditions?

(A) The animals prefer to be in the dark, regardless of other conditions.
(B) The animals prefer to be in the light, even in dry conditions.
(C) The animals prefer to be in the dark when other conditions are equal.
(D) The animals express no preference in any condition.

378. Given the data, which do you think the animals would prefer?

(A) Moist and dark conditions
(B) Acid and dark conditions
(C) Dry and lighted conditions
(D) Moist, acid, and dark conditions

379. Of the following, one substance is NOT found within the gallbladder. Which is that one substance?

(A) α-amylase
(B) Lipase
(C) β-galactosidase
(D) Nucleases
(E) Peptidases

380. When a person enters chronic renal failure, which of the following would be likely to be observed?

(A) Increased erythrocyte production
(B) Generalized edema
(C) Hyponatremia
(D) Hypouremia
(E) Alkalosis

381. Which of the following is NOT a section of the large intestine?

(A) Cecum
(B) Transverse colon
(C) Sigmoid colon
(D) Vermiform appendix
(E) Duodenum

382. Intrinsic factor allows the absorption of vitamin B_{12} within the

(A) stomach.
(B) transverse colon.
(C) jejunum.
(D) ileum.
(E) vermiform appendix.

383. Nephrons can be found within which kidney region(s)?

(A) Renal cortex and pelvis
(B) Renal pelvis and medulla
(C) Renal pyramid and cortex
(D) Bowman's capsule
(E) Renal medulla

384. Which of the following is NOT a function performed by the liver?

(A) Lipid metabolism
(B) Production of albumin and some blood clotting proteins
(C) Carbohydrate metabolism
(D) Storage of water-soluble vitamins
(E) Storage of iron and vitamin B_{12}

385. When a gallstone is passed, where does it go?

(A) Bladder
(B) Duodenum
(C) Pancreas
(D) Liver
(E) Stomach

386. Amylase is released into the digestive tract in which region(s)?

    (A) Large intestine and vermiform appendix

    (B) Mouth and stomach

    (C) Esophagus

    (D) Small intestine and mouth

    (E) Large intestine

387. Which of the following represents the correct sequence of the passage of urine in a nephron?

    (A) Bowman's capsule → loop of Henle → distal tubule → collecting tubule

    (B) Loop of Henle → Bowman's capsule → distal tubule → collecting tubule

    (C) Bowman's capsule → loop of Henle → collecting tubule → distal tubule

    (D) Collecting tubule → proximal tubule → distal tubule → Bowman's capsule

    (E) Bowman's capsule → distal tubule → loop of Henle → proximal tubule

388. Bile is composed of which of the following combinations of substances?

    (A) Cholesterol, bile salts, HCl

    (B) Water, bilirubin, cholesterol

    (C) Bile salts, nitrogenous wastes, bilirubin

    (D) Amylase, glycogen, bile salts

    (E) Trypsin, bile salts, glycogen

389. Which of the following is NOT a function of the material(s) produced by parietal cells within the stomach?

    (A) Activation of pepsinogen

    (B) Killing of microorganisims

    (C) Formation of gastric mucus

    (D) Absorption of vitamin B_{12}

    (E) Denaturation of proteins

390. Salivation is important for the digestive process. Which of the following is NOT true about saliva or salivation?

    (A) Saliva contains antibodies and lysozymes.

    (B) A typical adult produces about one liter of saliva daily.

    (C) Saliva contains mucin, amylase, and bicarbonate.

    (D) Saliva is composed of about 99.5 percent water.

    (E) There are four pairs of salivary glands: parotid, submandibular, pharyngeal tonsils, and sublingual.

391. The term "countercurrent multiplier mechanism" refers to

(A) the laboratory technique used to evaluate protein concentration in urine.

(B) the mechanism by which lipids are absorbed within the intestinal tract.

(C) the mechanism used to create a concentration gradient within the loop of Henle.

(D) the mechanism used by the autonomic nervous system to control peristalsis.

(E) the model used within the stomach to produce significant quantities of HCl.

392. Which of the following is true concerning mechanisms involved within the loop of Henle?

(A) Water enters the urine in the descending portion.

(B) Sodium and chlorine leave the urine in the ascending loop.

(C) Water leaves the urine in the ascending portion.

(D) Proteins are absorbed back into the blood in both the ascending and descending portions.

(E) Water, sodium, and potassium leave the urine in the descending portion.

393. Which of the following is NOT descriptive of the small intestine?

(A) Nutrient absorption takes place within the small intestine.

(B) Epithelial brush border cells are involved in carbohydrate digestion.

(C) The lumen is lined with plica covered with villi to increase adsorption.

(D) Peristalsis of the small intestine is under autonomic control.

(E) Digestion in the small intestine begins in the jejunum.

394. Alcohol intake increases urination by

(A) simply increasing water intake as well.

(B) interfering with the function of ADH.

(C) altering the ion balance in the nephrons.

(D) blocking the readsorption of proteins, thus altering fluid balance.

(E) interfering with the production of ADH in the adrenals.

395. What is the physiologic response when someone increases their water intake?

 (A) The adrenals increase the rate of water readsorption in the kidneys.
 (B) The hypothalamus and anterior pituitary decrease the rate of water readsorption in the kidneys.
 (C) The pancreas releases insulin to increase sugar and water uptake by all cells.
 (D) The glomeruli in the kidneys decrease the effectiveness of retaining proteins in the blood, increasing urinary output.
 (E) The autonomic nervous system increases the rate of sweat production as a means of maintaining fluid balance.

396. Which of the following is true about the absorption of carbohydrates?

 (A) Polysaccharides are broken down into simple sugars in the intestinal lumen, which then passively diffuse into the lymph.
 (B) Proteins are broken down into monosaccharides in the intestinal lumen, which are then brought into the epithelial cells by active transport.
 (C) Complex carbohydrates are brought into epithelial cells by active transport, which then enter the lymph by facilitated diffusion.
 (D) Simple sugars enter epithelial cells by active transport, exit these cells by facilitated diffusion, then enter capillaries by simple diffusion.
 (E) Since the sugar concentration is highest in the intestinal lumen and lowest in the blood, simple diffusion is all that is needed to get the sugar into the blood.

397. The sequence of the process needed for lipid absorption is

 (A) digestion by lipases → emulsification by bile salts → formation of chylomicrons → secretion by epithelial cells.
 (B) formation of chylomicrons → secretion by epithelial cells → movement into lymph → digestion by lipases.
 (C) emulsification by bile salts → formation of chylomicrons → digestion by lipases → movement into lymph.
 (D) digestion by lipases → formation of chylomicrons → movement into lymph → adsorption of micelles.
 (E) emulsification by bile salts → digestion by lipases → formation of chylomicrons → secretion by epithelial cells.

398. The kidneys have a role in all of the following EXCEPT

 (A) excretion of wastes and toxic substances.
 (B) maintaining body fluid pH.
 (C) contributing to homeostasis.
 (D) disposal of bilirubin through the urine.
 (E) maintaining fluid balance and blood pressure.

399. What is the function of the septal cells found within the alveoli of the lungs?

(A) They provide immune surveillance, protecting the lungs from infection.

(B) They secrete surfactants.

(C) They comprise the bulk of the alveolar cells involved in gas exchange.

(D) They serve as a barrier between the circulatory system and the respiratory system.

(E) They serve to remove dust and dirt particles within the lungs.

400. The proper sequence of structures that inspired air encounters en route to the circulatory system is

(A) pharynx → larynx → trachea → bronchi → bronchioles → alveoli.

(B) alveoli → larynx → pharynx → bronchioles → bronchi → trachea.

(C) pharynx → trachea → larynx → bronchi → bronchioles → alveoli.

(D) trachea → pharynx → larynx → bronchioles → bronchi → alveoli.

(E) pharynx → bronchi → bronchioles → trachea → alveoli → larynx.

401. Which of the following is the best description for inspiratory reserve volume?

(A) The amount of air within the lungs at rest

(B) The amount of air remaining in the lungs after forced exhalation

(C) The maximum amount of air that can be brought into the lungs

(D) The difference between the amount of air in the lungs at rest and the amount brought in by the use of muscles

(E) The amount of air expelled by the muscles after being at rest

402. Boyle's law is important in understanding the breathing mechanism. It states that

(A) for any given temperature, air pressure remains constant at sea level.

(B) blood pressure and atmospheric pressure are directly correlated.

(C) there is an inverse relationship between pressure and volume for a given amount of air.

(D) gas flow from the atmosphere to the blood and from the blood into the atmosphere is independent.

(E) the flows of the different atmospheric gases are all linked.

403. The component(s) of the conductive segment of the respiratory system that lack(s) cartilage include(s) the

(A) pharynx.

(B) trachea and bronchi.

(C) pharynx, trachea, and bronchi.

(D) trachea and bronchioles.

(E) bronchioles.

404. The autonomic control of breathing is centered in the

(A) AV node.
(B) medulla oblongata.
(C) cerebellum.
(D) hypothalamus.
(E) respiratory gyrus of the cerebrum.

405. What is the fate of CO_2 acquired in the tissue capillaries when it enters the blood?

(A) More than 90 percent of it enters erythrocytes, and about 25 percent of that binds to hemoglobin.
(B) All of it remains in the plasma as dissolved CO_2.
(C) Less than 10 percent remains in the plasma as CO_2, while the remainder disassociates into H^+ and HCO_3^-.
(D) All of it is converted to HCO_3^- within the erythrocytes, which is then released into the plasma by passive diffusion.
(E) About 25 percent returns to the tissues by passive diffusion as the blood returns to the lungs; the remainder is exhaled.

406. Which of the following conditions generally does NOT interfere with gas exchange within the alveoli?

(A) Pulmonary tuberculosis
(B) Chemically induced pneumonia
(C) Emphysema
(D) Bacterial pneumonia
(E) Lung cancer

407. If the atmosphere contains 78 percent nitrogen and 21 percent oxygen, about what percentage of the total blood gases is nitrogen?

(A) 78 percent
(B) 28 percent
(C) 67 percent
(D) Less than 2 percent
(E) 95 percent

408. The movement of respiratory mucus helps protect the respiratory tree. Which of the following is true about this mechanism?

(A) All of the mucus is swept upward in order to be swallowed or spit out.

(B) Mucus below the larynx is swept downward, and mucus above the larynx is swept upward.

(C) Mucus above the pharynx is swept downward, and mucus below the pharynx is swept upward.

(D) Movement of the mucus is random to prevent attachment to the epithelium by respiratory pathogens.

(E) The movement of the mucus helps assure that both the upper and lower respiratory tracts remain sterile as maintained by macrophages.

409. Which of the following provides the best description of the anatomy of the lungs?

(A) Three left lobes and two right lobes resting on the diaphragm, all surrounded by pleural membranes.

(B) Three right lobes and two left lobes surrounded by pleural membranes, resting upon the diaphragm.

(C) Two left lobes and three right lobes surrounding the heart, all surrounded by pleural membranes.

(D) Three left lobes and two right lobes surrounding the heart and resting on the diaphragm, all surrounded by pleural membranes.

(E) Three right lobes and two left lobes surrounded by pleural membranes, surrounding the heart and all resting on the diaphragm.

410. Stimulation of chemoreceptors can affect lung function. Which of the following does NOT occur when alveolar CO_2 levels get too high?

(A) Bronchodilation increases airflow to the alveoli.

(B) The respiration rate increases.

(C) The elevated CO_2 levels produce the yawning reflex.

(D) The pO_2 levels drop proportionately.

(E) The rate of gas exchange in the alveoli increases.

411. The respective partial pressures (in mm Hg) for oxygen (pO_2) and carbon dioxide (pCO_2) in the tissues are

(A) $pO_2 = 40$ mm; $pCO_2 = 45$ mm.

(B) $pO_2 = 40$ mm; $pCO_2 = 100$ mm.

(C) $pO_2 = 100$ mm; $pCO_2 = 60$ mm.

(D) $pO_2 = 100$ mm; $pCO_2 = 40$ mm.

(E) $pO_2 = 40$ mm; $pCO_2 = 20$ mm.

412. Irritation of which of the following areas does NOT produce a coughing reflex?

(A) Larynx
(B) Oropharynx
(C) Primary bronchi
(D) Trachea
(E) Secondary bronchi

413. Chronic obstructive pulmonary disease (COPD) is defined as a condition representing a loss of more than 50 percent of expected breathing capacity. Which of the following is NOT included in this definition?

(A) Chronic asthma
(B) Chronic bronchiolitis
(C) Pulmonary emphysema
(D) Chronic bronchitis
(E) Bacterial pneumonia

414. The nasal turbinates have several roles within the respiratory system. Which of the following is NOT one of those roles?

(A) To moisten the air entering the lungs
(B) To recover water that might be lost during exhalation
(C) To cool the air entering the lungs
(D) To carry air to the olfactory centers
(E) To trap dust and larger infectious materials

415. Materials exit the blood and enter the urine in the

(A) Bowman's capsule.
(B) proximal convoluted tubule.
(C) ascending portion of the loop of Henle.
(D) medullary pyramid.
(E) efferent arteriole.

CHAPTER 11

The Musculoskeletal System

Passage 10: Questions 416–420

Two independent groups of researchers centered in eastern Colorado were studying the effects of climate change on animal populations. One group was monitoring *Canis latrans*, the common coyote, and the other was monitoring *Cynomys ludovicianus*, the black-tailed prairie dog. Eventually they each learned of the other's work, and they subsequently got together to compare the data that they had both collected over a period of nearly a decade. When the data were correlated and normalized, the following graph was constructed.

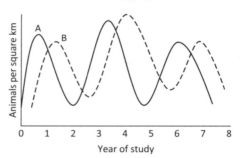

416. Can a correlation between the two data sets be observed?

    (A) Yes, regardless of whether the study areas overlapped

    (B) No, no correlation is observed.

    (C) Yes, assuming that the study areas were congruent

    (D) No, even if the areas overlapped

417. Assuming that a correlation exists, what is the most likely explanation?

    (A) The peaks and valleys correlate with average temperatures.

    (B) The peaks correlate with increased rainfall.

    (C) The peaks correlate with excessive winter conditions.

    (D) The valleys indicate increased predation.

418. Assuming that average rainfall in inches per year was added to the Y axis, what would that curve most likely look like?

    (A) Similar rises and falls immediately preceding curve A
    (B) A fairly flat curve running roughly parallel to the X axis
    (C) Similar rises and falls immediately following curve B
    (D) Similar rises and falls roughly running between curves A and B

419. What additional information would be most disruptive to the interpretation of these data?

    (A) Accidental combination of data concerning two different species of coyote
    (B) A loss of data collected during six months of year 4
    (C) Identification of curve A as the coyote and curve B as the prairie dog
    (D) A methodological error that missed 30 percent of the animals in both populations

420. Which is the most likely explanation for the curves represented?

    (A) Increased numbers of predators caused them to turn upon themselves.
    (B) The prey species improved its ability to elude predators.
    (C) The increased numbers of prey species intimidated the predators into leaving the study area.
    (D) The increased number of predators decreased the number of prey as a result of increased predation.

421. Thin filaments of the muscle cell are composed of all of the following EXCEPT

    (A) actin.
    (B) troponin.
    (C) tropomyosin.
    (D) myosin binding sites.
    (E) myosin.

422. If half of the calcium present in a muscle cell leaked out of the cell into the surrounding tissue, what would occur?

    (A) Muscle strength would increase.
    (B) Signal strength from the neuron to the muscle would increase.
    (C) The action potential within the adjacent neuron would be dampened.
    (D) The force of contraction of the muscle cell would decrease.
    (E) The muscle cell would contract with its normal strength.

423. Bone tissue is best associated with the storage of

(A) calcium.
(B) water.
(C) sodium.
(D) proteins.
(E) potassium.

424. Which of the following correctly describes smooth muscle?

(A) Smooth muscle tissue is localized only along the digestive system.
(B) Smooth muscle cells are striated and under involuntary control.
(C) Smooth muscle tissues are best associated with bony structures.
(D) Smooth muscle tissues provide for long-term slow contractions.
(E) Smooth muscle contractions are under voluntary control.

425. Which of the following are NOT bones of the skull?

(A) Maxilla and mandible
(B) Palatine and sphenoid
(C) Tarsals and metatarsals
(D) Parietal and occipital
(E) Ethmoid and zygomatic

426. Which of the following muscle combinations works synergistically?

(A) Sartorius and hamstring
(B) Biceps and triceps
(C) Pectoralis major and trapezius
(D) Quadriceps and biceps
(E) Hamstring and gastrocnemius

427. Which of the following is NOT true concerning the vertebrae?

(A) There are seven cervical vertebrae.
(B) The coccyx is composed of seven fused bones.
(C) The lumbar region is located below the thoracic region.
(D) The sacrum connects the coccyx to the lumbar vertebrae.
(E) The vertebrae protect portions of the CNS.

428. A fibrous joint is best described as

(A) immovable.
(B) a joint similar to the knee or elbow.
(C) slightly movable.
(D) a joint similar to that which connects the sternum to the adjacent cartilage.
(E) highly movable.

429. The best concept related to a sarcomere is that it

(A) is the place where a bone attaches to muscle tissue.
(B) is another name for a muscle cell.
(C) contains the postsynaptic receptors of a muscle.
(D) stores calcium needed for muscle contraction.
(E) is the contractile unit of the myofibril.

430. Which of the following is NOT a primary function of the skeletal system?

(A) It provides support for movement.
(B) It is essential for cellular metabolism.
(C) It is the primary reservoir for calcium and phosphate.
(D) It provides for hematopoiesis.
(E) It protects the organs.

431. The sarcoplasmic reticulum is

(A) protected by the skull.
(B) essential for muscle contraction.
(C) involved in protein synthesis and transport.
(D) a cellular joining structure that provides for muscle fiber integrity and strength.
(E) essential in the transport of ATP from the mitochondria to the contractile unit in muscle cells.

432. Spongy bone is best associated with

(A) bone loss.
(B) the structure of the diaphysis.
(C) the medullary cavity.
(D) the proximal epiphysis.
(E) the periosteum.

433. Which of the following is NOT closely associated with the knee?

(A) Ligaments
(B) Patella
(C) Fibrous joint
(D) Meniscus
(E) Femur

434. Which of the following is used to power muscle cells immediately after the initial supply of ATP is exhausted?

(A) Glucose
(B) Creatine phosphate
(C) Fatty acids
(D) Glycogen
(E) Protein

435. The _____ is the connective tissue that contains osteoclasts.

(A) epiphysis
(B) yellow marrow
(C) haversian canal
(D) compact bone
(E) periosteum

436. The muscles best associated with peristalsis of the digestive system are controlled by

(A) the parasympathetic nervous system.
(B) the cerebrum.
(C) the sympathetic nervous system.
(D) both the sympathetic and the parasympathetic nervous systems.
(E) the cerebrum and the cerebellum.

437. During adolescent development, bones elongate by

(A) forming bone tissue just under the joint cartilage.
(B) deposition of spongy bone within the marrow cavity.
(C) forming bone tissue under the cartilage epiphyseal plate.
(D) deposition of dense bone along the marrow cavity.
(E) deposition of collagenous fibrocartilage at the ends of the marrow cavity.

438. Which of the following is the best description of a tendon?

(A) A connective tissue that encloses synovial fluid
(B) A bone-derived tissue that connects bone to bone
(C) A highly vasculated tissue that connects bone to muscle
(D) A collagenous material that connects bone to bone
(E) A connective tissue that connects bone to muscle

439. The thin filament of a sarcomere is composed primarily of

(A) titin.
(B) tropomyosin.
(C) actin.
(D) troponin.
(E) myosin.

440. Osteoarthritis differs from rheumatoid arthritis in that the former

(A) is caused by wear, while the latter is caused by infection.

(B) retains the overall integrity of the joint, while the latter produces permanent deformation.

(C) is initiated by mechanical mechanisms, while the latter is an autoimmune disorder.

(D) affects primarily synovial joints, while the latter primarily affects fibrocartilage.

(E) involves adjacent ligaments, while the latter does not.

441. Cardiac muscle cells, when grown in the lab in petri plates, begin to beat in a synchronized fashion when they make contact with each other. Why might this be so?

(A) The cells start to form nerve connections between themselves.

(B) The cells release ATP into the surrounding medium in a synchronized fashion.

(C) The cells release calcium ions, which synchronize contractions, into the surrounding medium.

(D) The cells connect to each other by gap junctions upon making contact.

(E) When one cell starts to contract, any cell in contact with that cell responds to the sudden motion as a physically gated stimulus.

442. What is the sequence of the repair of a bone following fracture?

(A) Callus forms → hematoma forms → osteoclasts remove fragments → osteoblasts replace bone material.

(B) Osteoclasts remove debris → osteocytes form haversian canals → hematoma forms → callus forms.

(C) Hematoma forms → callus forms → osteocytes form haversian canals → osteoblasts replace bone material.

(D) Callus forms → osteoclasts remove debris → hematoma forms → osteoblasts form haversian canals.

(E) Hematoma forms → callus forms → osteoclasts remove debris → osteoblasts replace bone material.

443. Which of the following is NOT true about the human rib cage?

(A) Ribs 8–10 are known as false ribs.

(B) All ribs are attached to thoracic vertebrae.

(C) The spaces between the ribs are called intervertebral spaces.

(D) Ribs 11 and 12 are not connected to the sternum.

(E) The rib cage is considered part of the respiratory system.

444. Which of the following is true about bone–skeletal muscle interrelatedness?

(A) Muscles connect through tendons to relatively immobile origins.
(B) Muscles produce motion by pushing against the tendon origin.
(C) Joints rotate when synovial pressures increase suddenly.
(D) Muscles connect through tendons to relatively immobile insertions.
(E) Muscles connect to a single bone at both ends via collagenous fibrocartilage.

445. The axial skeleton consists of all of the following EXCEPT the

(A) skull.
(B) ribs.
(C) vertebrae
(D) sternum.
(E) femurs.

446. A person with McArdle's disease has a deficiency in glycogen storage. How would this disease manifest itself?

(A) Rapid onset of fatigue during exercise
(B) Adult-onset type II diabetes
(C) Muscle atrophy because of inability to contract
(D) Very short stature and increased bone density
(E) Rapid cartilage degeneration and early-onset arthritis

447. The structures analogous to the tibia and fibula are the

(A) carpal and metacarpal.
(B) radius and ulna.
(C) humerus and scapula.
(D) sacrum and coccyx.
(E) clavicle and scapula.

448. Which of the following is probably NOT appropriate for someone with osteoporosis?

(A) Calcium supplementation
(B) Moderate exercise
(C) Estrogen replacement for women
(D) Contact sports
(E) Stretching

449. The muscle that bends the backbone is the

   (A) rectus abdominis.
   (B) latissimus dorsi.
   (C) gluteus maximus.
   (D) external oblique.
   (E) serratus anterior.

450. Which of the following is true about a condition known as scoliosis?

   (A) It involves the pathology produced by improper incorporation of silicon into bone tissue.
   (B) It is the result of the improper closure of the fontanels during infancy.
   (C) It is the improper lateral curvature of the spine.
   (D) It is an allergic response to cold.
   (E) It is the result of bone stenosis.

451. What is meant by the term "cartilaginous bones"?

   (A) Bones that articulate with cartilage
   (B) A condition caused by the lack of ossification
   (C) Ossified bones with inappropriate cartilaginous deposits
   (D) Bone structure surrounded by a layer of cartilage
   (E) Bone development within a cartilage framework

452. What actually happens following a period of oxygen debt?

   (A) Oxygen levels in the blood rebound to above preexercise levels.
   (B) Conversion of lactic acid to glucose.
   (C) ATP conversion of creatine phosphate.
   (D) Oxygen levels in the muscles rebound to above preexercise levels.
   (E) Creatine phosphate levels rebound to above preexercise levels.

453. What is the reason that organisms thermoregulate?

   (A) In order to maintain fluid balance.
   (B) It is the key to maintaining electrolytes within physiologic requirements.
   (C) Cellular enzymes function within a narrow temperature range.
   (D) The immune system and healing work best within a species-specific range.
   (E) Excessive temperatures produce elevated metabolic rates with excessive nutritional requirements.

454. In what way, if any, is the endocrine system involved in oxygen delivery to muscles?

(A) The kidneys produce erythropoietin.
(B) The heart produces atrial natriuretic peptide.
(C) Cholecystokinin is produced within the digestive system.
(D) Lack of oxygen triggers the release of prostaglandins.
(E) The endocrine system is not involved.

455. Which of the following is NOT descriptive of red muscle?

(A) Rich in mitochondria
(B) High capillary density
(C) Rich in myoglobin
(D) Fast twitch
(E) Best for sustained exertion

456. Why do some insects, such as wasps, continually move their wings even when walking?

(A) The wings act as a warning to potential predators.
(B) They must keep their flight muscles warm.
(C) The wings are associated with venom production.
(D) The wings are involved in keeping the body cool.
(E) It appears to have no discernible function.

457. Which of the following is NOT associated with the maintenance of posture?

(A) Myotatic reflex
(B) Knee-jerk reflex
(C) Flexor reflex
(D) Deep tendon reflex
(E) Stretch reflex

458. What protein is found at the highest levels in bone tissue?

(A) Elastin
(B) Fibronectin
(C) Keratin
(D) Actin
(E) Collagen

CHAPTER 12

Reproduction and Development

459. When males differ in appearance from females, this difference is referred to as

(A) sexual dimorphism.
(B) a primary sexual characteristic.
(C) polymorphism.
(D) being monoecious.
(E) primary selection.

460. Which of the following is the tissue usually involved in an ectopic pregnancy?

(A) Vagina
(B) Uterine tube
(C) Perimetrium
(D) Endometrium
(E) Ovary

461. The proper sequence of the development of the sperm is

(A) primary spermatocyte → secondary spermatocyte → spermatid → Sertoli cell.
(B) spermatid → primary spermatocyte → secondary spermatocyte → Sertoli cell.
(C) secondary spermatocyte → primary spermatocyte → spermatogonium → spermatid.
(D) spermatogonium → primary spermatocyte → secondary spermatocyte → spermatid.
(E) Sertoli cell → spermatogonium → secondary spermatocyte → primary spermatocyte → spermatid.

462. A human female has about _____ primary oocytes at birth, of which about _____ will be released by ovulation.

(A) 10,000; 500
(B) 500,000; 500
(C) 20,000; 200
(D) 100,000; 100
(E) 5,000; 500

463. Which of the following is the best description of a polar body?

(A) The mature female gamete
(B) A haploid cell that produces primary oocytes
(C) A degenerate cell resulting from meiosis
(D) A haploid cell in a secondary follicle that is released at ovulation
(E) A diploid cell that gives rise to the secondary oocyte

464. Sperm are formed in the

(A) epididymis.
(B) seminiferous tubules.
(C) prostate gland.
(D) vas deferens.
(E) bulbourethral gland.

465. The follicular phase of the menstrual cycle includes

(A) the uterine proliferative phase, the menstrual phase, and the rise of estrogen and LH.
(B) the menstrual phase, the secretory phase, and the rise of progesterone.
(C) ovulation and the rise of progesterone and estrogen.
(D) the rise of LH, FSH, estrogen, and progesterone.
(E) the rise of progesterone and the secretory phase.

466. The purpose of the acrosome on the tip of sperm cells is to provide

(A) the energy to burrow through the zona pellucida.
(B) the molecular sensors for chemotaxis to the ovum.
(C) enzymes that permit tunneling through the zona pellucida.
(D) the energy required to power the flagellum for movement toward the ovum.
(E) protection for the sperm in the hostile environment encountered en route to the ovum.

467. Components of human sperm include all of the following EXCEPT

(A)   microtubules.
(B)   flagellum.
(C)   endoplasmic reticulum.
(D)   acrosome.
(E)   mitochondria.

468. Testosterone is produced by

(A)   Sertoli cells in the seminiferous tubules.
(B)   spermatogonia within the seminiferous tubules.
(C)   the prostate.
(D)   the bulbourethral gland.
(E)   interstitial cells of the seminiferous tubules.

469. Which of the following hormones plays no role in a mother's lactation following birth?

(A)   Oxytocin
(B)   Estrogen
(C)   Progesterone
(D)   Prolactin
(E)   Testosterone

470. The luteal phase of the menstrual cycle is best associated with

(A)   progressively increasing FSH and LH levels.
(B)   the secretory phase of the uterine cycle.
(C)   menses and uterine proliferation.
(D)   a spike of estrogen, LH, and FSH.
(E)   ovarian follicle maturation.

471. Identify the component that would NOT be grouped with the others.

(A)   Epididymis
(B)   Prostate
(C)   Urethra
(D)   Vas deferens
(E)   Ureter

472. Which of the following serves as the ultimate regulator of FSH and LH in males?

(A) The interstitial cells of the testes
(B) The anterior pituitary
(C) The Sertoli cells of the testes
(D) The hypothalamus
(E) None of these; males produce neither LH nor FSH

473. What is the genetic composition of the polar body prior to the second meiotic division?

(A) Aneuploid
(B) Diploid
(C) Triploid
(D) Haploid
(E) The polar body is fully degenerate and contains no DNA.

474. Why is the Papanicolaou test (Pap smear), a method that is almost 70 years old, still preferred for the diagnosis of cervical cancer over the more specific and sensitive PCR test for HPV?

(A) An abnormal Pap smear is more predictive than the detection of just any HPV in cervical tissue.
(B) HPV is not linked to cervical cancer, but only to genital warts.
(C) The Pap smear is much cheaper and requires no technician time.
(D) The available vaccine for HPV produces PCR false positives.
(E) The Pap smear is actually being replaced by PCR for HPV.

475. Why is endometriosis often associated with infertility?

(A) It reduces the effects of LH.
(B) It blocks FSH receptors, interfering with the menstrual cycle.
(C) The fragmentation of the uterus produces scarring that block implantation.
(D) The cause is uncertain.
(E) The pelvic pain that is most associated with it prevents sexual activity.

476. The proper sequence of stages in preembryonic development is

(A) fertilization → cleavage of blastomeres → morula → blastocyst.
(B) cleavage of blastomeres → fertilization → morula → blastocyst.
(C) fertilization → blastocyst → morula → cleavage of blastomeres.
(D) morula → cleavage of blastomeres → fertilization → blastocyst.
(E) fertilization → blastocyst → cleavage of blastomeres → morula.

477. Which of the following is NOT a tissue derived from the embryonic ectoderm?

(A) Tooth enamel
(B) Posterior pituitary gland
(C) Skin epidermis
(D) Retina of the eye
(E) Thymus

478. Which is the correct sequence of the development of the CNS during embryogenesis?

(A) Notochord → neural groove → neural fold → neural tube
(B) Neural groove → neural fold → neural tube → notochord
(C) Notochord → neural tube → neural fold → neural groove
(D) Neural fold → neural groove → notochord → neural tube
(E) Neural groove → neural fold → notochord→ neural tube

479. Which of the following is the best description of the allantois?

(A) The remnants of the membranes and placenta
(B) The extraembryonic membrane that supports fetal development
(C) The vessel that carries the blood from the placenta to the fetus
(D) The extraembryonic membrane that forms the bladder
(E) The vessel that carries the blood from the fetus to the placenta

480. Identical twins are a result of

(A) double fertilization of a single ovum.
(B) separate fertilization of two different ova.
(C) fusion of two separately fertilized ova.
(D) division of a single fertilized ovum into two zygotes.
(E) division of a single ovum, with each being separately fertilized.

481. Which of the following is NOT a tissue derived from the embryonic mesoderm?

(A) Digestive tract mucosa
(B) Bone marrow
(C) Gonads
(D) Lymph vessels
(E) Connective tissue

482. Which of the following cell types does NOT originate within the neural crest?

(A) Neurons
(B) Lymphocytes
(C) Epinephrine-producing cells of the adrenal glands
(D) Epidermal pigment cells
(E) Glial cells

483. When humans develop *in utero*, the fingers of the hand are initially connected by weblike tissue that usually disappears prior to birth. What is it called when this doesn't happen?

(A) Polydactyly
(B) Apoptosis
(C) Cytokinesis
(D) Dyslysis
(E) Syndactyly

484. Marked jaundice in the infant at birth is a sign of

(A) Rh incompatibility with the mother.
(B) an autoimmune disorder.
(C) an ABO mismatch with the mother.
(D) an Rh mismatch with the mother.
(E) the infant inheriting the father's tissue type.

485. Which of the following is NOT a tissue derived from the embryonic endoderm?

(A) Sweat glands
(B) Anterior pituitary
(C) Muscle tissue
(D) Lung alveoli
(E) Thyroid gland

486. Cells differentiate during fetal development based on signals from other cells in proximity to them. Which of the following is NOT included in the signal response system model?

(A) A signal transport or translation mechanism
(B) A lipid synthesizing mechanism
(C) A signal protein
(D) A specific receptor protein
(E) A response that produces a gene regulatory product

487. A newborn infant has an immature immune system but is initially protected by

   (A) antibodies passed on from the mother in her breast milk.
   (B) T_H cells passed on from the mother through the placenta.
   (C) antibody-producing cells acquired from the umbilical cord during the birth process.
   (D) maternal macrophages occupying fetal lymph nodes.
   (E) antibodies passed on from the mother through the placenta.

488. Which of the following is NOT a correct pairing of extraembryonic membranes and their function?

   (A) Amnion—produces cushioning fluid for the fetus
   (B) Myometrium—helps form the placenta
   (C) Allantois—helps form the umbilical cord
   (D) Yolk sac—initially forms fetal blood cells
   (E) Chorion—assists in gas exchange between mother and fetus

489. During fetal development, at which point can a heartbeat initially be detected?

   (A) Month 3
   (B) Week 4
   (C) Week 8
   (D) Month 5
   (E) Month 4

490. When fingers initially form *in utero*, they are connected by skin "webbing." Yet at birth, this webbing is no longer present. Why is this?

   (A) There are no blood vessels present in the webbing, so the cells die off.
   (B) The buildup of fetal urine within the amnion removes these cells.
   (C) As the fetus starts to move the fingers, the thin web tissue tears and degrades.
   (D) The web cells undergo programmed apoptosis.
   (E) Maternal antibodies in the amnion attack and remove these temporary cells.

491. What is the distinction between protostomal and deuterostomal development?

   (A) Protostomes gastrulate the mouth opening first, while deutrostomes gastrulate the anus first.
   (B) Deuterostomes bypass the blastula stage, while protostomes do not.
   (C) Deuterostomes gastrulate the mouth opening first, while protostomes gastrulate the anus first.
   (D) Protostomes bypass the blastula stage, while deuterostomes do not.
   (E) Protostomes have a blind gut, while deuterostomes do not.

492. Keratinized squamous epithelium describes cells

    (A) lining the lumen of the small intestine.

    (B) lining the interior of the stomach.

    (C) covering a nerve bundle.

    (D) that comprise tendons.

    (E) that make up the skin.

493. Certain cell types are found only in specific tissues, while others are scattered throughout the body. In which of the following is a goblet cell NOT found?

    (A) Trachea

    (B) Eyes

    (C) Kidneys

    (D) Intestine

    (E) Bronchioles

494. The concentration of spot desmosomes, tight junctions, and gap junctions is highest with which of the following?

    (A) Skin

    (B) Blood

    (C) Fibroblasts

    (D) Neurons

    (E) Alveoli

495. What significant event begins to trigger cellular differentiation in the blastocoel stage of embryonic development?

    (A) An increased rate of cellular division

    (B) A large increase in the cellular volume of all cells

    (C) A sharp temporary drop in metabolic rate

    (D) The first onset of gluconeogenesis

    (E) The formation of tight junctions

496. Which of the following is NOT part of the human conceptus?

    (A) Amnion

    (B) Embryo

    (C) Umbilical cord

    (D) Yolk sac

    (E) Chorion

497. At which point following fertilization does implantation within the uterus normally take place?

(A) Day 3
(B) Day 9
(C) Day 2
(D) Day 6
(E) Day 1

498. A condition in which an ovum, after fertilization, forms a nonviable and undifferentiated cell mass that mimics a pregnancy is a(n)

(A) miscarriage.
(B) ectopic pregnancy.
(C) chorionic pregnancy.
(D) molar pregnancy.
(E) stromal pregnancy.

499. Can a child's cells reside in the body of its mother?

(A) No; they have no mechanism for entry.
(B) Yes; they gain entry during the mixing of the mother's and the child's blood in the birth process.
(C) Yes, but they trigger an immune response and are eliminated within weeks of birth.
(D) Yes, and they are responsible for most chronic autoimmune diseases in women.
(E) Yes, and these cells can even be passed on to subsequent children.

500. What does the term *tetragametic* refer to?

(A) This is a person with the genetic composition of two once-separate individuals.
(B) This is the process whereby armadillos always have litters of four.
(C) This refers to the genetic composition of fraternal twins.
(D) This refers to the result of the meiosis of a single mother cell.
(E) This refers to the genetic composition of quadruplets.

ANSWER KEY

Chapter 1: Amino Acids and Proteins

1. **(B)** Enzymes are globular proteins with catalytic functions. As such, they lower the energy of activation for a specific biochemical process converting one or more reactants into one or more products. Thus, option A can be eliminated because enzyme density has no relevance. Option D can be eliminated because one would expect the curves to be inverted from what appears. Option C can be eliminated because the units used, μL/sec, would require a defined concentration to be valuable.

2. **(A)** Options B and C can both be eliminated because they reflect enzyme activity well below and well above enzymatic possibility (from 40°C below zero to 140°C above zero, respectively). This being true, option D can also be eliminated. This leaves option A as the most reasonable choice, indicating the activities of three enzymes over three different pH ranges.

3. **(C)** Option A can easily be eliminated, as the data would be a single point, not a range as in the figure. Option B can be eliminated because one would expect the curves to be much more complex rather than mere peaks. Options C and D should be inverses of each other, with D being the opposite of what is observed.

4. **(B)** Option D can be eliminated from consideration because the experimental data reflected reactivity to light, not the emission of light. Option A can be eliminated because the units used represent pressure, which is irrelevant to these data. Option C would be appropriate only if it were used on the axis labeled A.

5. **(D)** The lower the energy level, the longer the wavelength, and red light has longer wavelengths than blue light. Option A is the exact opposite of true, as is B, where pigment E absorbs, not reflects, the green light in the middle of the range. If option C were correct, the absorbance curve would be higher at each end and lower in the middle.

6. **(B)** Some inhibitors bind enzymes at other than the active site, but these are identified as allosteric inhibitors. A poison is an inhibitor that irreversibly binds and permanently deactivates an enzyme. While option B does not describe what a competitive inhibitor does, the fact remains that it cannot be processed at the active site, making this choice the correct one.

7. **(E)** Bacteria normally do not reproduce or metabolize faster at higher body temperatures. Fever does not block bacterial protein synthesis; if it did, fever would always be effective in halting bacterial growth. Option E is correct because an elevated body temperature causes all bacterial enzymes to function at less than the optimal rate, thus reducing the growth rate of the bacteria and giving the body a better chance to clear the infection.

8. (E) Cofactors are normally separate molecules from the enzyme. While the additional molecular size would affect the enzyme, it would not permanently disable it because, as soon as the modified substrate is removed from the reaction, the enzyme could act upon the unmodified substrate.

9. (D) Complement is a complex of normally inactive proteins circulating in the blood. When activated, a complex known as C1 begins a cascading series of reactions that cleave the inactive forms of these proteins to active forms one after another, ultimately producing an attack complex that drills holes through the cell membrane, causing lysis.

10. (B) Plasmapheresis is the process of removing plasma from the body, separating out protein fractions, and returning the remaining plasma components to the blood. The proteins normally sought for removal are those that are associated with clotting the blood, to be administered to hemophiliacs.

11. (B) When the letter "C" is followed by a number and is used in relation to the blood, it refers to the protein components of the complement cascade, identified as C1–C9. The primary function of complement is the targeting and lysis of invading cells such as bacteria. This means that the lack of C4, one of the key proteins in the cascade, would prevent the lysis and destruction of bacteria producing an infection.

12. (E) Assays that require free uncoagulated cells include a complete blood count, hematocrit, and a differential stain. Measuring complement proteins can be done on either plasma or serum. However, you could not measure clotting time on blood collected in a material that would prevent clotting.

13. (B) The active site of an enzyme is the location that physically interacts with the substrate and product molecules. Other molecules that physically resemble these can also fit into the active site and, when doing so, inhibit proper enzyme function.

14. (C) By definition, all amino acids have only one R-group. The Miller-Urey experiments actually abiotically synthesized many more than just 20 amino acids. Only the L-forms are used in synthesis, but both D- and L-forms exist in cells. The 20 are the only ones that attach to the tRNAs used in protein synthesis as directed by the codons of the genetic code.

15. (D) While the 20 amino acids used in protein synthesis are essential because protein synthesis will fail if they are not present, regardless of how often they are needed, an "essential" amino acid is one that cannot be synthesized by an organism and thus must be acquired in its diet.

16. (E) Proteins are used for energy as well as for metal storage, enzymatic catalysis, transport of substances such as oxygen, and defense against invaders, such as by antibodies. Micells, however, are composed only of lipids, which spontaneously aggregate in water.

17. (A) β-pleating is one of the two basic secondary structures formed by proteins as they begin to fold after emerging from the ribosome. This pleating can be likened to the shape seen with corrugated steel roofing. The strand of consecutive amino acids forms a repetitive up-down configuration that can repetitively fold back and forth, forming the sheeted structure. This pleating is stabilized by hydrogen bonding between the adjacent strands, just as they also provide for the annealing of the two antiparallel complementary strands in DNA.

18. (C) Proteins will spontaneously fold into their final tertiary configuration based on the combined interactions of the R–side chains and will tend to assume the shape requiring the least energy. However, under conditions of physical or thermal stress, some proteins will tend to congregate into inactive clusters. Chaperones are present to reduce the effects of these aggregates and to help maintain proper protein function.

19. (A) The group of amino acids that present with nonpolar and uncharged R-groups includes alanine, isoleucine, leucine, methionine, phenylalanine, proline, tryptophan, and valine. These include both aliphatic and aromatic R-groups.

20. (D) All amino acids contain an amine group ($-NH_2$, as in *amino*), a carboxyl group ($-COOH$, as in carboxylic *acid*), a single hydrogen atom, and a unique defining side chain, all attached by covalent bonds to a single central carbon atom. Only two of the amino acids used in protein synthesis contain sulfur: methionine and cysteine.

21. (B) Some proteins, such as heat shock proteins, function at elevated, but still narrow, temperature ranges. Disulfide bridges, formed between the two sulfur-containing amino acids methionine and cysteine, are much less susceptible to these environmental factors and are especially adept at linking multiple protein chains into a final quaternary form, such as that seen in an antibody molecule, which has two heavy and two light chains.

22. (C) Most proteins function best under optimal physiologic conditions, which include a rather narrow temperature, salinity, and pH range. Any conditions outside of this range alter the shape of the protein and, by altering the shape, also alter the function. When this shape alteration is irreversible, the protein is permanently denatured.

23. (D) The double leaflet structure of a membrane is maintained by the presence of water at both the interior and exterior surfaces, which forces the hydrophobic fatty acids toward the central region of the membrane. The presence of porin proteins is maintained by regions rich in hydrophobic amino acids that are similarly repelled by the water at the surfaces.

24. (A) The group of amino acids that present with polar R-groups includes asparagine, cysteine, glutamine, serine, threonine, and tyrosine. These polar side chains allow hydrogen bonding with adjacent partially polar water molecules.

25. (E) Immunoelectric focusing is performed in a gel with a pH gradient. Proteins are inserted, and an electric current is applied. Depending on the isoelectric point (pI) of a protein, the surrounding hydrogen ion concentration will cause the protein to move toward one electrode or the other until neither the carboxylate groups are protonated nor the ammonium groups are deprotonated. At this point, the protein ceases to migrate and concentrates within a detectable band in the gel.

26. (E) Serum protein electrophoresis separates serum proteins based on size and net charge at a specified pH. Serum proteins will separate into five regions: albumin, $\alpha 1$ globulins, $\alpha 2$ globulins, β globulins, and γ globulins. The proteins will continue to migrate within the gel as long as the current is applied and will not focus as in IEP. After completion, the concentration of each band is determined by scanning densitometry.

27. (C) Enzymes vary widely in size, complexity, and the need for cofactors or coenzymes, while antibodies are basically the same four-chain configuration. But both the active site of enzymes and the binding sites of antibodies have nearly infinite variety and rely on the initial weak binding of the substrate (or antigen) to trigger a much higher affinity-induced fit, which then ensures the specificity of the function.

28. (B) A mildly reducing thioglycolate solution breaks disulfide bridges in hair. The strands of hair are then shaped as desired, changing which cysteines are physically adjacent. This repositioning is then made "permanent" by forming new disulfide bridges with a mildly oxidizing solution of hydrogen peroxide.

29. (A) Peptide bonds are formed during protein synthesis by combining the carboxyl group of one amino with the amine group of another, which releases a molecule of water (dehydration) when completed. This bond is maintained in a flat structure by resonance stabilization.

30. (D) A cofactor is an inorganic molecule that must be present in order for the active site of an enzyme to assume its proper form. If such a cofactor is an organic molecule such as a water-soluble vitamin, then it is referred to as a coenzyme. Both function by interacting with the enzyme at some location other than the active site. A noncompetitive inhibitor interferes with the enzyme function by allosteric inhibition.

31. (C) A competitive inhibitor is known as such because it competes with the substrate for access to the active site, and the higher its concentration, the more likely it will be that it rather than the substrate will fill the active site. Thus continually increasing the concentration of a competitive inhibitor will continually decrease enzyme activity. This is not true for a noncompetitive inhibitor, where a maximum inhibition level can be reached, beyond which additional inhibitor will have no further effect.

32. (E) Deamination (or decarboxylation, a similar process) is the removal of the amine (or carboxyl) group of an amino acid, in this case lysine. An enzyme that catalyzes the removal of any group is known as a lyase.

33. (B) To ligate means to join together. In the case of enzyme function, a ligase is one that forms a covalent bond between two molecules, thus joining them together. The enzyme that completes the DNA replication process by joining together Okazaki fragments is known as DNA ligase.

34. (A) Cells utilize enzymes, which are large globular protein catalysts, to catabolize organic materials. Enzymes function by greatly reducing the energy or activation required to break or form chemical bonds, thus avoiding the requirement for random thermal energy to do so.

35. (D) Some enzymes are synthesized in an inactive form so that they can be manufactured in one location but utilized in another. Additionally, some may become activated only when they are needed and under the correct conditions. These precursor forms are known as zymogens.

36. (C) Many proteins have a nonenzymatic purpose, and many of these are associated with membrane function. One of these vital functions is the regulated movement of substances across a membrane that otherwise could not do so without the required transport protein. Uniport is the motion of something in one direction, symport the motion of two different substances in the same direction, and antiport the motion of two things in opposite directions. In all three cases, the expenditure of energy may or may not be required.

37. (B) It takes energy not only to synthesize amino acids (in those organisms that can), but also to form the peptide bonds in the ribosome during the elongation phase of translation. Since proteins contain many carbon-to-carbon bonds, these bonds can be broken to release at least some of the energy it took to form them, and thus proteins can be used for storage with the same energy content per gram as carbohydrates.

38. (E) The complete catabolism of proteins and amino acids results in the normal buildup of the nitrogen contained within the released amine groups. This excess is normally exported from the cell and transported to a filtering organ such as a kidney, where the excess is secreted as urea or uric acid.

39. (A) Based on the original work on enzyme binding by Victor Henri of France, Leonor Michaelis of Germany and Maud Menten of Canada began to investigate the mechanism of action of the enzyme invertase. Their now famous equation defining enzyme rate specifics was published in 1913.

40. (C) Standard temperature and pressure must be considered only in reactions involving gases, although temperature and pH must also be considered. The reaction rate forward will increase with increasing substrate concentration and will quickly reach a maximum only when there is a marked excess of substrate to enzyme.

41. (B) Protein-based molecular motors involve the movement of the motor along the surface of a specific substrate. The best example of this is the movement of a myosin fiber along the actin fiber in the contractile element of a muscle. However, the action is facilitated by the conversion of ATP to ADP + Pi (releasing chemical energy) into movement (performance of mechanical work).

42. (E) An enzyme's structure is dependent on the primary, secondary, and tertiary structures assumed during synthesis, and these are dependent on the mRNA codes transcribed. However, as with other genes, the initial DNA sequence may be mutated or have multiple versions or alleles. In the case of enzymes, different structural versions, or isoenzymes, may exist, and each may vary in its rate kinetics.

Chapter 2: Molecular Biology

43. (E) Deoxyribonucleic acid (DNA) is a polymer of nucleosides. Each nucleoside is composed of a nucleobase coupled to a pentose sugar. If the sugar is ribose, the resulting polymer is RNA; if it contains deoxyribose, it is DNA. All sugars contain carbon, hydrogen, and oxygen. Thus, all DNA contains these and the nitrogen of the nucleoside. The only element listed that is not included here is iron.

44. (B) Restriction endonucleases cut through both strands of DNA, but usually at very specific sequences. Most of these sequences are palindromes. Thus, the complementary sequence for option A, AGCT, would read (in the opposite direction) AGCT, making this palindromic. The same is true for options C, D, and E. However, it is not true for option B, where GACGAC would read in a similar manner GTCGTC.

45. (C) One of the peculiarities of most restriction enzymes is that they do not cut straight through, but rather make a jagged cut a base or two apart on the two strands in the same locations within the palindromic sequence. This produces an overhang of single-stranded bases. These overhangs are called "sticky ends" because they will spontaneously reanneal with any DNA cut with the same restriction enzyme.

46. (D) Replication of both eukaryotic and prokaryotic DNA begins the origins of replication (ORI). This melting is normally accomplished by enzymes that separate the two complementary strands, such as helicases. Enzymes that prevent supercoiling are called topoisomerases. Sigma (σ-) factors identify where a polymerase binds to DNA. Ligation is accomplished by DNA ligase.

47. (A) If the DNA triplet AAC is transcribed, the corresponding complementary sequence on the mRNA would be UUG. The UUG sequence represents the codon that would be used within the ribosome. Looking at the table providing the genetic code, it can be determined that UUG codes for "Leu." The correct answer is therefore leu(cine), option A.

48. (B) Any mutation that affected growth on a plate containing glucose only must involve the glucose operon and would have nothing to do with lactose. This eliminates all options other than B.

49. (C) Option B can be eliminated, as it excludes changes in lactose utilization. Both options A and C are possible, but a mutation such as that described in A might very well produce silent or neutral expression that would still allow the cell to utilize lactose. Option C, on the other hand, would completely disrupt the *lac* operon by preventing the close association of bacterial RNA polymerase with the *lac* promoter, thus preventing transcription.

50. (C) The *lac* operon is inducible, which means that it is normally repressed but can become induced under certain conditions. For this operon, the presence of both lactose and cAMP are needed for induction. The most obvious way to convert a normally repressed gene to one that is unregulated or constitutively expressed is to prevent the binding of the repressor to the operator region. This makes option C the only reasonable choice.

51. (D) The production of the pigment is determined by the presence of genetic material in the form of DNA. This DNA may be genomic or episomal; it is usually in the form of a plasmid, although it can be contained within a phage as well. Here, any of the three options might account for the introduction of pigment-encoding DNA, so option D is the best choice.

52. (A) All three sources of the DNA (a phage, a DNA fragment, and a plasmid) are small enough to pass through a 0.1-μm (100-nm) filter, so option D is not the best choice. Option B might be helpful in the identification of mRNA by annealing to the poly-A tail, but this works only with eukaryotes that posttranscriptionally modify the message. Option C would be totally ineffective. Option A, on the other hand, could result in the precipitation of the proteins of the phage capsid and their separation from the other two materials.

53. (C) A silent mutation means that the resulting protein is identical in function to the original, or wild type. Also of little consequence are mutations found within most noncoding regions. However, any mutation that changes any highly conserved sequence would nullify its purpose. Thus, if that occurred within the TATAAT box of a critical enzyme, that gene could no longer be expressed and the cell would probably die.

54. (E) DNA ligase is an enzyme associated with DNA replication, not degradation, so option B can be excluded from consideration. The enzymes identified in options C and D are also polymerases associated with synthesis, so they can be ignored. β-lactamase (option A) is an enzyme best associated with the ability of bacteria to resist the effects of certain antibiotics, not viruses. Thus, only option E remains.

55. (B) The initiation of bacterial transcription is controlled by recognition proteins identified as σ-factors. These factors serve to select the genes that should be expressed under those same conditions for optimal cellular functioning. If the conditions in which the cell is living change dramatically, different σ-factors will be expressed, which then allow for the rapid shift in metabolism that is required for the cell to survive.

56. (D) RNA transcription takes place only where DNA might be present, which includes the nuclear region of bacteria or its eukaryotic equivalent of the nucleus. However, both mitochondria and chloroplasts, thought to have once been bacterial symbiotes of a primeval host cell, are also capable of transcribing and expressing their own genes using their own genetic code.

57. (C) Among the evidence for the Endosymbiotic Theory are the facts that chloroplasts and mitochondria have their own separate genome, bacterialike DNA polymerases, and bacterialike ribosomes. The ribosomes of the eukaryotic cell are found only within the cytosol, although they are commonly closely associated near the endoplasmic reticulum (ER).

58. (D) Base pairing is most commonly associated with the double-stranded structure of DNA. However, RNA is also capable of base pairing with itself, forming regions of double-strandedness. DNA is found within bacteria, mitochondria, and chloroplasts, so option E can be ignored. Option B reverses the correct association, so it is wrong. Option C is actually true for both DNA and RNA. So only option D remains as true.

59. (A) Helicase is first involved in the separation of the two strands of DNA. Topoisomerases are involved in preventing supercoiling. DNA polymerase is responsible for the actual manufacture of the new strand after reading the base sequence on the template strand. Later, when rejoining separate Okazaki fragments in lagging-strand synthesis, DNA ligase is finally involved.

60. (A) Ribosomes are clusters of several strands of rRNA intertwining through ribosomal proteins. Option C is one aspect included in option E, and both are associated with mRNA in eukaryotes. Option D involves converting nucleotide sequences from an RNA to a DNA form. Option B identifies processes involving protein modifications following translation.

61. (E) Eukaryotic DNA contains extensive noncoding regions interspersed between those that contain codes used for the production of proteins. Following transcription, the newly manufactured RNA is processed by splicesomes to remove these introns and rejoin the essential coding regions. This shortened strand is then further modified at both the 3′ and 5′ ends before being released from the nucleus for translation in the cytosol.

62. (B) The concept of wobble involves the third position of the codon. This position is the one that permits the greatest latitude in changes without necessarily changing the resulting amino acid to be inserted during translation, and thus that is most likely to not change the essential nature of the resulting protein. Only option B reflects a single change in the codon at this third position.

63. (B) During the first phase, initiation, the ribosome engages mRNA. The second phase, elongation, lasts the longest, as each tRNA brings its appropriate amino acid into the ribosome for addition to the elongating protein. During the final phase, termination, a stop codon is encountered and the ribosome disassociates.

64. (C) Hybridization between two strands of nucleic acid is highly dependent upon the proper orientation of the various bases to each other, and G-C combinations contain three hydrogen bonds, while A-T pairs contain only two. While the sequences found in both options C and E would hybridize under certain conditions, option E has several mismatches that would reduce the binding strength.

65. (A) The photons within ultraviolet (UV) wavelengths contain appreciably more energy than those of visible light. Depending on that energy level, UV light either will cause the production of thymine dimers or will nick and degrade the DNA. Degraded DNA will, if not repairable, induce the cell to undergo apoptosis and die.

66. (C) DNA is DNA, regardless of what organism or virus may be its source. That means that it is of uniform dimensions throughout its length. DNA is composed of deoxyribose and contains thymine, while RNA is composed of ribose and contains uracil. Both groups of organisms share the same genetic code, although it is slightly different in mitochondria and chloroplasts.

67. (A) The Shine-Dalgarno sequence is a sequence of bases found within the noncoding leader section of mRNA. This sequence is vital during the initiation phase of translation, as it provides the recognition signal used by the ribosome to properly orient the mRNA with the rRNA of the ribosome. It ensures that the start codon will be in the proper position to initiate the translation process.

68. (D) The self-cleaving ability of some RNAs, known as ribozymes, provides evidence of biologic catalysts in a nonprotein form existing prior to the development of proteins.

69. (E) mRNAs are exported out of the nucleus for translation within the cytosol. These proteins are then escorted back into the nucleus, where they begin to associate with strands of rRNA transcribed from DNA regions within the nucleolus. These subassemblies are then exported back out into the cytosol for final assembly as ribosomes to participate in translation.

70. (E) Fidelity means accuracy in the copying or reproduction process, and there are more than 50 genes associated with DNA replication and DNA repair to ensure accuracy. DNA polymerase makes mutational mistakes about every 1,000 bases, but it has an exonuclease proofreading function that allows it to correct these errors. This improves its fidelity by another three orders of magnitude.

71. (B) The question describes a polyadenylation (poly-A) sequence, such as is seen at the 3' end of mRNA exported from the nucleus for translation into a protein. rDNA codes for both ribosomal proteins and rRNA and has no such characteristics. cDNA is similar in structure to rDNA, except that it lacks introns. Polyadenylation is a normal part of post-transcriptional modifications, so the poly-A tail is not a waste product.

72. (D) While DNA ligase is used in genetic engineering to finalize the construction of modified plasmids, it is also normally present in the replisome, and both are active in the lagging-strand synthesis of DNA replication. Restriction enzymes are universally used to cut apart DNA containing genes of interest.

73. (D) A previous question mentioned that G-C base pairings involve three hydrogen bonds, while A-P base pairings involve only two. Options B and C can be eliminated because they do not form, as they are noncomplementary. Option A, and its RNA equivalent option E, indicate that just two bonds are involved. This means that option D is the correct choice.

74. (A) Lagging-strand synthesis is much more involved than leading-strand synthesis and requires the function of multiple enzymes in a complicated sequence. DNA ligase is required to remove the nicks in one of the DNA strands only following lagging-strand synthesis.

75. (C) The Pribnow box identifies a highly conserved sequence in prokaryotes that is required for RNA polymerase to recognize and bind to DNA in the promoter region in order to initiate transcription. This sequence, which is found 10 base pairs prior to the starting point of transcription, is 5'-TATAAT-3'. Its equivalent in eukaryotes, again indicating the binding site for DNA-dependent RNA polymerase, is 5'-TATA-3'.

76. (B) Option D describes a theoretical process called "conservative replication," which was hypothesized as a possible replication method before the confirmation of the actual semiconservative mechanism described in option B.

77. (E) Genes are generally identified by a three-letter code, usually printed in italics, and refer to the function with which they are best associated. For example, the genes associated with the bacterial manufacture of the amino acid tryptophan are identified as *trp*E, *trp*D, *trp*C, *trp*B, and *trp*A. It is thus easy to link *rec*A to option E, *rec*ombination repair.

78. (E) All three forms are capable of forming short regions of double-strandedness, are chemically identical and contain uracil in lieu of thymine, and are exported out of the nucleus and are present within the ribosome during protein synthesis. The one thing that distinguishes mRNA from the other two forms is that mRNA contains the code necessary for the production of proteins, while this is not true for rRNA and tRNA.

79. (A) While salts can be used to inhibit hydrogen bonding between DNA strands, once they are added, they will continue to do so, limiting their effect to a single cycle. DNA polymerase does not melt the complementary DNA strands; that function is accomplished by helicase within the cell. Normal double-stranded DNA will melt at 95–100°C, which is accomplished during the heating phase of the PCR process.

80. (C) While DNA fragments could be separated by the technique presented in options A, B, and D, this would be cumbersome and inefficient. The technique presented in option E does not exist. One of the techniques most commonly used in the genetics laboratory is the Southern blot. Before the DNA fragments can be identified or used for cloning, the simplest separation method preceding these is agarose gel electrophoresis.

81. (B) Options A, D, and E all state or imply that this transfer is relatively energy-independent. However, the formation of peptide bonds, which store energy, requires the addition of sufficient energy to activate the linkage. Option C refers to catalytic action, but option B specifically identifies the energy expense, so it is the preferred answer.

82. (E) The production of RNA requires an RNA polymerase enzyme. Option D refers to an enzyme that degrades, not synthesizes, RNA, and so it also can be excluded. Without knowing which of the two remaining choices is right, one would be better off guessing the choice that was probably identified later in the discovery process, making option E the better choice.

83. (C) The human genome project made some astounding discoveries, among which was the amount of human DNA that actually codes for human components. When added up, all noncoding regions amount to more than 98 percent of the human genome, meaning that only about 2 percent actually codes for "us." Two percent of 1.8 meters is 3.6 cm, making option C the correct one.

Chapter 3: Genetics and Evolution

84. (A) Eukaryotes and prokaryotes have both genomes and genotypes. A genotype best represents the genetic content of expressed genes, usually focusing on individual genes and comparing their content from individual to individual. The genome represents the entire content of the nucleus (for eukaryotes) or nucleosome (for prokaryotes) of an individual.

85. (E) Banding patterns produced with Giemsa stain after trypsin digestion of cells arrested in metaphase reveal that there are 22 homologous pairs and one nonhomologous pair (the sex chromosomes) in male nuclei.

86. (C) Kleinfelter's syndrome results when one of the gametes that produced the zygote contains an extra X chromosome produced by nondisjunction during gametogenesis.

87. (B) In the ABO blood group system, an individual's blood group is controlled by one set of alleles. Homozygous individuals may be blood group A, B, or O. Heterozygous individuals may be blood group A (AO), B (BO), or AB. This indicates codominance.

88. (E) During meiosis, a primary diploid cell undergoes DNA replication and becomes tetraploid. While it is in this state, homologous chromosomes align tetrads and undergo intentional but random gene rearrangements in a process known as crossing over. After this recombination, the tetraploid cell undergoes two sequential reduction divisions, with each cell becoming haploid.

89. (D) All of these options represent genetic disorders. Cystic fibrosis, however, is caused by a defect in an ion channel protein controlling sodium transport. This results in excessive mucus secretion in the lung, which leads to bacterial infections and fatal pneumonia.

90. (B) Mitosis is a process in which an individual cell replicates its DNA with high fidelity and then divides into two genetically identical daughter cells. When a single diploid cell replicates its DNA and then divides into four genetically distinct daughter cells, it is called meiosis.

91. (E) If both parents are heterozygous, then the four blood types will be equally represented.

92. (A) The convention used in the construction of Punnett squares is that dominant, codominant, or incomplete dominant alleles are indicated by a capital letter. Recessive alleles are indicated by a small letter.

93. (D) Gametes contain only one copy of each chromosome, so their genetic content is half that of the somatic cells, meaning that these haploid cells contain a total of only 23 chromosomes.

94. (A) Any change in a DNA sequence is a mutation, and these changes in genotype may or may not be observed in the phenotype.

95. (B) X-linked refers to a gene whose allele is present on the X chromosome. These genes follow the same rule of dominance as alleles found on the autosomes except that expression may be dependent on whether the alleles are expressed in male or female individuals.

96. (B) Tay-Sachs disease is an autosomal recessive condition. Someone with Tay-Sachs disease suffers muscle degeneration because of a defect in a lipid-producing enzyme that leads to excessive lipid buildup in the CNS.

97. (C) An unmatched allele on a sex chromosome best describes a hemizygous condition, not a locus. A gene product that affects another gene product indicates epistasis, not a locus. While the term *locus* can refer to any gene on any chromosome, it refers to the actual physical location on a chromosome, which makes option C the best choice.

98. (C) If one animal has brown hair and another black, then their genotypes (and therefore their genetic sequences) also differ, eliminating both options A and E. Additionally, because the animals differ in gene expression, they must differ in allelic composition, also eliminating option D. While both animals may or may not have the same parents, they definitely have the same brown hair, as they both possess the same dominant allele. This makes option C a much better choice than B.

99. (D) Expression of genes on one chromosome can affect the expression of genes on a different chromosome by epistasis, making option C incorrect. If such genes are on different chromosome pairs, then they must be autosomal, eliminating option A. Genes that are on separate chromosomes will never be linked (eliminating option D). Although genes on separate chromosomes might show up in the same gametes (making option B a possibility), they very well might not because they will always sort independently (making option D the best choice).

100. (B) A series of fragile chromosomes or any other genetic disorder may result in the expression of a syndrome, but they are not the syndrome itself. This eliminates both options A and C. A syndrome always has some description, so, although it may be poorly defined, it will never be undefined, eliminating option D. A syndrome might be a series of conditions that are uncommon, but the word is derived from Greek roots that mean "running together," as in symptoms or signs that appear to run together in the course of a certain disease process. This makes option B the best choice.

101. (A) Mitochondria are thought to be remnants of some symbiotic bacteria that took up residence in host cells eons ago. Evidence for this includes the fact that they contain their own DNA, which has primarily prokaryotic sequences (eliminating option E). Just as a collection of bacteria in a colony displays some heterogeneity in genetic content, so we also find multiple mitochondrial genomic variations within an individual cell. This eliminates option D. Mitochondria are found only in the cytosol of eukaryotic cells (eliminating option B) and never in a prokaryote (eliminating option C). Option A is the best choice, although there is some recent evidence that some paternal mitochondria sneak in every once in a while.

102. (C) The term *mutation* can be used to describe either genotype or phenotype changes in an organism, but the former is more accurate. Changes in the DNA may be small, such as point mutations in which one nitrogenous base is substituted for another. They may also be slightly larger and more likely to have a greater effect on the cell, such as a frame-shift mutation produced by the removal or insertion of one or more bases, or they may be extensive, such as a translocation or inversion mutation. Changes in the DNA that occur within an intron, even extensive ones such as deletion or inversion mutations, could produce the situation described in the question. This eliminates options B, D, and E. A silent mutation is one in which the coding DNA changes, but the resulting protein is identical to the wild type in amino acid sequence, most likely because the mutation produced a change in the third position of the codon (the wobble position). That means that option A can also be true and can be eliminated. What cannot be true, however, is that this could be a neutral mutation because, by definition, it produces a change in the protein sequence, making option C the only correct choice.

103. (D) The key to understanding this problem is that test crosses are always done with individuals that are homozygous recessive. The purpose of the test cross is to determine whether the genotype of an individual displaying the dominant characteristic is homozygous (say, GG) or heterozygous (Gg). Crossing this unknown with an individual that is known to be homozygous recessive (gg) will result in a ratio of either all displaying the dominant characteristic, because all of the offspring of GG × gg will be heterozygotes (Gg), or a ratio of 1:1 because the cross of Gg × gg will produce 2 × Gg and 2 × gg. This makes option D the correct answer.

104. (E) If the daughter is expressing the recessive gene, then she must be homozygous recessive. If the gene expression is sex-linked, this means that it is found only on the X chromosome. Option A cannot be correct because it would mean that the allele she inherited from her father was dominant, and option C is wrong for the same reason. Option B is incorrect because if the mother is heterozygous, then there is a 50:50 chance that any sisters would inherit the dominant trait, and option D is also incorrect, as the same would be true for any brothers. Only option E is correct.

105. (D) While blood group AB$^+$ is known as the universal receiver because any individual with that blood type lacks natural antibodies that would cause a transfusion reaction, this has not been subject to selection pressure and offers no evolutionary advantage. This allows the elimination of option B. Turner syndrome is the result of a female individual having only one X chromosome. This syndrome includes, among many other common characteristics, dysfunctional gonads and sterility. This also offers no selective advantage, making option C a poor choice. Down syndrome, or trisomy 21, is a result of an individual's receiving an extra twenty-first chromosome. Having this extra chromosome carries with it an increased risk for obesity, frequent ear infections, thyroid dysfunction, and heart defects, none of which confer any advantage, making option E another poor choice. Color blindness, option A, is a characteristic that confers neither positive nor negative advantages and can also be eliminated. Option D is different. The sickle cell mutation, when present in a homozygous individual, carries with it a high selection pressure against the person with it. On the other hand, individuals that are homozygous normal are very susceptible to death from malaria. Individuals that are heterozygous, however, are partially protected from malaria and have a reduced chance of sickle cell crisis because they also carry a normal allele. Option D is the correct choice.

106. (B) The ABO blood group inheritance is controlled by codominance. Thus, a person with type O blood is simply homozygous recessive, and a person with AB blood is heterozygous codominant A and B. This eliminates both options A and C from further consideration. Both options D and E are possible with simple dominance, eliminating them as well. Option B, however, is a classic case of codominance, where the heterozygous condition is a blend of the dominant and recessive characteristics.

107. (D) There are 64 codon positions in the standard genetic code. Three of these are stop codons, which carry release factors to the ribosome during protein synthesis instead of essential amino acids. These release factors cause the termination of translation and the release of the protein from the ribosome. If a specific tRNA were no longer available, then the result would be similar to a nonsense mutation that causes early termination of a protein, but instead of occurring in just one protein, it would occur in all or almost all proteins. This would clearly disrupt most cellular functions. This is why option D is the best choice.

108. (D) Meiosis produces gametes that are subject to Mendel's laws. One of these deals with independent assortment. Under this law, the four genes identified would sort independently of each other. Simply multiplying the probability of each allele times those of the others will determine the number of different possible combinations. Normally this would be $2 \times 2 \times 2 \times 2$, for a total of 16. However, the gene identified as B is present in only one allelic form, changing the calculation to $2 \times 1 \times 2 \times 2$, for a total of 8, making option D the correct choice.

109. (C) During meiosis, when the chromosomes are arranged in tetrads during prophase I, random but equivalent amounts of DNA are exchanged between the chromatids in a process called crossing over. Because genes that are physically located close together have a greater chance of moving together, and thus being inherited together, they are referred to as being linked. Linkage is a relative term, but in general, the closer the genes, the more likely they are to move together. The centimorgan is a calculated value representing the likelihood of genes crossing over together and is thus an approximate value for their actual distance apart on the chromosome. While there are huge variations because of the wide differences in the distribution of noncoding DNA, on average, one centimorgan is about one million base pairs in humans. This makes option C the correct choice.

110. (B) Epistasis is when the expression or effects of one gene are influenced by one or more modifier genes. The mechanism may be at either the genotypic or the phenotypic level. Option D can easily be discarded because the effect described is a normal expression of different alleles for the same gene. Options A and C are unlikely, as both can be explained by sex-linked inheritance. While option E may well be true, option B presents a much more likely scenario and is the best choice.

111. (C) Option E describes a condition of separation, not segregation, and can be ignored. Option A is incorrect because the separation is not complete; if it were, most gametes would vary from having one and only one copy of every gene. Option B is also incorrect for the same reason. Option D presents the description of the effects of Mendel's Second Law, that of independent assortment, and is therefore incorrect. Option C correctly identifies the principle of Mendel's First Law.

112. (E) Hemophilia is a condition in which the ability of the blood to form clots is impaired. This may be due to a problem with thrombocyte levels or, more likely, a deficiency in one of the clotting proteins. The condition is of historical note because it afflicted many of the royal houses of European countries through their frequent marriages of relatives. What was observed was that male children were much more commonly afflicted with this life-threatening disorder than female children. This is now known to be the case because the women in these families were often heterozygous for the affliction gene, which was found on the X chromosome. Since males have only one X chromosome, if they inherited the bad gene, they were afflicted. This is a classic case of an X-linked recessive inheritance pattern, making option E the correct choice.

113. (C) Since the plumage color mutation must have occurred prior to the observation of the color in this population, it must have occurred before the researchers discovered it. This means that option C is the correct one.

114. (C) Both options B and D would be expected to increase the percentage of the red group, not decrease it, as the data show, and can thus be eliminated. While option A might be considered a possibility, it would take many generations for it to originate in a single mating pair, and it would have to increase, not decrease, reproductive success in their progeny. Option C is the most likely possibility, with perhaps some effect linked to the color change increasing resistance to the virus.

115. (D) Although there are precedents for options A, B, and C, none of the data presented can infer any one of these over the others or even suggest which might be true. Thus, no conclusion can be drawn as yet concerning any behavioral linkage.

116. (B) None of the data presented support option D, so it can be removed from consideration. The preference expressed by the females is prezygotic, not postzygotic, so option C can also be eliminated. The 2 percent bias is not insignificant and could well produce such a population change over enough time, so option A is less likely. Option B, on the other hand, identifies a condition consistent with the data where a homozygous recessive trait would be increasing in a population.

117. (D) That a change in population is being observed eliminates option A from consideration. The change is occurring within the same population within the same area, so option B is similarly out. Because two populations appear to be emerging, option C is also gone. The remaining choice, option D, could very well explain a possible speciation event by emerging behavioral isolation.

118. (A) Trisomy 21 identifies a condition in which a child is conceived with a sperm or ovum that was the result of nondisjunction during gametogenesis. This resulted in every cell derived from the zygote (that is, all cells of the body) containing an extra chromosome 21 in its nucleus. Since this condition does not present unusual antigens on cells, they will not be targeted for destruction by apoptosis following immune surveillance, making option D incorrect. Additionally, while trisomy 21 generally leads to diminished mental development, it is not a fatal condition, making option B a poor choice. Gene therapy, as currently envisioned, offers the possibility of adding an effective gene into cells that lack it, but cannot be used to remove entire chromosomes. Option C is therefore a poor choice as well. Although trisomy 21 could be detected in every cell of a body, this is not the case with cancers, which are clearly clones of abnormal cells. This makes option E incorrect. Since transformed cancer cells lack the ability to control their own growth, these cells evidence abnormal distributions of DNA in their nuclei, making both cancer cells and cells with trisomy 21 identified as aneuploid. Option A is correct.

119. (B) There are three alleles for the ABO blood system. Because the A and B antigens bear a close resemblance to naturally occurring sugar combinations that occur in food, individuals with these blood types will develop natural antibodies against the opposite blood type. This means that a person with type A blood cells will develop anti-type B antibodies, and vice versa. A person with type AB blood will produce neither antibody, while a person with type O blood cells, which lack both antigens, will naturally develop antibodies that will attack any cell with either A or B antigens, and this obviously includes AB cells as well. The Rh factor is independent of this, although low levels of anti-Rh factor will develop in Rh-negative individuals. This all explains why a person who is AB positive is considered a universal acceptor because he possesses no antibodies that will attack transfused blood and can thus receive any blood type. This is also why someone with blood type O negative is considered a universal donor, because her cells lack all antigens that would agglutinate with antibodies that might be in a recipient's blood. Option A is incorrect because of the dilution effect of the donor's cells that would occur following transfusion. Having a protozoan parasite present in donated blood would not produce a transfusion reaction, although it might cause malaria later, eliminating option E. That Jim's blood has some antigens is indicated by its causing a reaction, and this eliminates option C. While option D might be true, option B is clearly the better choice.

120. (E) This question is not asking for the expected ratio of phenotypes, but the actual distribution of genotypes. It is also important to understand that the question requests the distribution after two test crosses, not just the first. The first test cross would result in a population that is entirely heterozygous. However, crossing GgHh × GgHh, while resulting in a phenotype distribution of 9:3:3:1, would result in the appearance of nine different genotypes. Five of these are represented only once, three of them are represented twice, and one, GgHh, is expected 5 out of 16 times. This makes option E the correct choice.

121. (B) In order to categorize the chromosome distribution within a cell, that cell must be observed during mitosis. In order to increase the likelihood of observing a full set of chromosomes, a substance is added to arrest the cell cycle during this stage. The nuclei are then squashed to disperse the chromosomes and stained with Giemsa stain to aid in the identification of pairs by both length and banding patterns. The substance that is most commonly used to arrest the cell cycle is colchicine, which inhibits the formation of the microtubules used to separate the chromosomes following metaphase. This makes option B the correct choice.

122. (C) A pathogenic condition is most commonly treated at the phenotypic level. This means that whatever physiological imbalances are being encountered, whether they be infectious, genetic, or chronic, can be either restored to normal or ameliorated by intervention. Genetic modalities can be offered if there is a genetic basis for the disease. Options A, B, D, and E all represent mechanisms that intervene at the genetic level. Only option C presents a change after genetic expression has occurred, making it the correct choice.

123. (A) Options B, C, and E can immediately be removed from consideration because only the male contributes the Y chromosome, and only one can normally be present in the zygote. The two possible combinations of X chromosomes from the female are XX or 0 (representing none present). If the male contributes an X chromosome, then the possible results of fertilization will be XXX and X0, which do not appear as an option. If the male contributes a Y chromosome, then the possible combinations become XXY and Y0, which are seen as option A, making it the correct choice.

124. (D) Karyotyping analysis requires nucleated cells. While this excludes erythrocytes in the blood, it does not do so for the leukocytes, which are the cells that are most commonly used for this process, as they are easily obtained by phlebotomy. While this is true for adults and children, it is much more difficult, and more risky, to obtain blood by venipuncture from a fetus *in utero*. This eliminates option B. A spinal tap not only would entail unacceptable risks, but would not be particularly efficient for harvesting cells, so option E is an especially poor choice. Both options A and C would collect mostly fully differentiated and nondividing cells, so they would not prove useful for this technique. The best method for fetal analysis is the collection of fetal cells sloughed free into the amniotic fluid by amniocentesis, making option D the best choice. It should be pointed out, however, that recent reports indicate that enough fetal cells can be found in the circulation of the mother's blood to permit this analysis on them.

125. (C) Sometimes the possession of an allele does not necessarily mean that that allele will be expressed. This is especially true for a defective gene that enters the population as an allele. Dominance is a condition in which the presence of one allele prevents the expression of another, not reflecting any difference in expression, so option A is incorrect. Epistasis involves multiple genes, not alleles, so option B is also an inappropriate choice. The Hardy-Weinberg law deals with constant gene frequencies, not variations of expression, so option D is a poor choice. In genetics, leakage refers to the flow of genes horizontally, or from one species to another, and has no application here, allowing option E to be ignored as well. Penetrance is the term used to describe differences between the number of individuals carrying a gene and the number expressing the gene. Option C is the best choice.

Chapter 4: Metabolism

126. (B) If there were any significant difference in the rate of incorporation of carbon-14, it would be measured as an increase above the baseline. Carbon dating is based on the assumption that the level of carbon-14 in the atmosphere remains constant, and that its incorporation into organic material ceases with the death of the organism, at which point there must be an irreversible decline in the percentage of total carbon. An increase to start with would thus be nonsensical, and option B is correct.

127. (A) The amount of carbon-14 in the atmosphere is very small compared to the normal amount of carbon-12. In any event, a two-day depletion of carbon-14 would simply imply that the plant died two days earlier than it otherwise did, and this difference is too small to be reliably detected.

128. (C) Without the presence of CO_2, which is required for carbon fixation, the plants would be incapable of growth, protein synthesis would cease, and the plants would die. Nitrogen, although freely available in inorganic form in the atmosphere and present in that form in all tissues, is inaccessible without conversion to organic form by bacteria.

129. (C) Although plants, as part of the harvesting of electrons and hydrogen ions from water during photolysis, release oxygen as a waste product, the amount released is inadequate to meet the needs of the mitochondria as a final electron acceptor in aerobic respiration and energy production. The plants would die for the same reason that humans would die without oxygen to breathe.

130. (B) As long as the level of atmospheric gases exceeds the level within plant cells, the partial pressure differential would be enough to permit the continued diffusion of the gases from outside to inside the cells, and thus they would function normally.

131. (D) The TCA cycle defines a process whereby a molecule of acetyl-CoA is fed into a looping series of reactions that consumes the molecule and restores the cycle for the input of the next one. For every two carbon atoms contained within the acetyl-CoA input, two molecules of CO_2, two molecules of ATP produced by substrate-level phosphorylation, three molecules of NADH, and one molecule of $FADH_2$ are kicked out.

132. (B) There are three conditions that define oxidation: (1) when a molecule gains an oxygen atom, (2) when a molecule loses an electron, or (3) when a molecule loses a hydrogen ion (proton). Oxidation is always coupled with reduction, that is, when one molecule is oxidized, another is reduced. Reduction is simply the opposite of oxidation. The conversion of NADH to NAD indicates a loss of a hydrogen ion, and thus oxidation.

133. (C) The maintenance of homeostasis requires the localized focusing of energy to maintain order. Cells must constantly consume energy to offset the loss of energy and organization as a result of the second law of thermodynamics.

134. (D) Energy is constantly required by any living organism because it must be used to constantly counter the degenerative effects of increased randomness; thus, option A is true. Energy is also required to "do work," which means to allow all cellular functions to continue, so options B and C are equally true.

135. (D) Glycolysis refers to the catalysis of glucose to pyruvate through this one primary cellular route. It takes five enzymatic steps to reduce glucose to two molecules of phosphoglyceraldehyde and five additional steps to rearrange the PGAL molecules to the structure called pyruvate. Thus, glycolysis involves 10 steps, making option D the true answer.

136. (A) When a high-energy electron is delivered to the electron transport system from NADH, it starts traveling down the chain at the flavoprotein FMN. Some energy from this electron is then used to pump a pair of hydrogen ions (H^+) from the matrix to the inner membrane space. The electron is then transferred to the second component, coenzyme Q, which repeats the same function. Thus, this latter component transfers both electrons and protons.

137. (E) Anaerobic respiration is defined as "an ATP generating process in which molecules are oxidized and the final electron acceptor is an inorganic molecule other than oxygen." Oxygen can act as a final electron acceptor like the other choices, but when it is used for that purpose, the result is known as aerobic, not anaerobic, respiration.

138. (B) This question is related to the previous one. The basis for identifying the form of respiration is always based on the substance that acts as the final electron acceptor in the process. If the final electron acceptor is oxygen or an inorganic ion, the process is considered aerobic or anaerobic respiration, respectively. The last possibility, the final electron acceptor being an organic molecule, defines fermentation.

139. (C) Lipids (oils or fats) contain 9 C per gram, while proteins and carbohydrates both contain 4 C each gram. Thus, if 6.5 g of protein is consumed, there are $6.5 \text{ g} \times 4 \text{ C/g}$, which equals 26 C available for use by the body. Thus, all options other than C are incorrect.

140. (B) The CO_2 generated in the tissues come from the metabolism of glucose, in which each of the six carbon atoms is used to produce this low-energy-containing waste gas.

141. (A) In eukaryotes, the electron transport system resides in the mitochondria. There, the high-energy electrons harvested from glucose are bled of their energy to drive the proton pumps. Bacteria are capable of oxidative phosphorylation, but they are prokaryotic in structure, and their electron transport system resides within their cell membrane, not within an organelle.

142. (D) This self-regulating mechanism is known as both end-product inhibition and feedback inhibition. The activation of this mechanism is produced by any buildup of pathway product.

143. (E) Energy is contained within all chemical bonds that hold a molecule together. Reactions that increase the molecule's size tend to increase that energy content, known as ΔG. Reactions that reduce molecular size tend to release energy; this is $-\Delta G$. These energy-releasing reactions are always exergonic and are also generally catabolic.

144. (C) The two strongest forms of chemical bonds are ionic and covalent, and the latter can be of either a polar or a nonpolar variety. The form of bond that holds together two complementary strands of DNA, which can be overcome with the simple heating of water, is the hydrogen bond.

145. (B) Each of the first three components of the electron transport chain captures enough energy from the donated electron to permit it to pump a pair of hydrogen ions from one side of the mitochondrial membrane to the other. Each pair then returns to its original place by passing through a molecule of ATP synthase, which, in turn, converts one molecule of ADP to ATP. Three pairs per electron thus produce three molecules of ATP by oxidative phosphorylation.

146. (A) Generally, the less saturated a lipid is, the greater the volume required by each molecule. Conversely, the greater the saturation, the more densely the molecules can pack together, thus requiring more heat to break them apart.

147. (D) The terms *autotroph* and *heterotroph* refer to sources of carbon. *Lithotroph* and *organotroph* refer to sources of electrons. A *phototroph* gets its energy from light, while a chemotroph gets its energy from organic molecules.

148. (C) Glucose is a hexose, as it is a carbohydrate containing six carbon atoms. Thus, any cell that extracts all the energy from a single molecule will produce, as a waste gas, six molecules of carbon dioxide containing single carbon atoms.

149. (A) A dehydration reaction, also known as dehydration synthesis, is one that releases a molecule of water in the process of forming a bond between two molecules. Whenever one of these molecules is a saccharide (sugar), then the resulting bond is called a glycosidic bond.

150. (B) Le Chatelier's principle briefly states that substances in equilibrium will be maintained in equilibrium unless standing conditions such as concentration, pressure, or temperature change, in which case the system will shift until a new equilibrium is achieved. The biological equivalent is homeostasis, where a biological system maintains internal cellular parameters under certain conditions. However, when those conditions change, the internal system will make adjustments until a new internal balance is attained.

151. (A) Milk is commonly pasteurized to eliminate pathogenic bacteria such as *Mycobacterium tuberculosis* or *Listeria* sp. that might sicken those who drink it. The classical process involves heating the milk to 63°C for 30 min, but this changes the flavor a bit, as do the faster methods of high-temperature, short-time (HTST) and ultra-high-temperature (UHT) processes. A cold process that retains most of the original flavor involves the addition of bacteriocidal hydrogen peroxide, which greatly reduces microbial content. This H_2O_2 is then converted back to water with the enzyme catalase.

152. (E) During electron transport in the mitochondrial membrane, pairs of hydrogen ions (H^+) are moved from the matrix to the intermembrane space side of the membrane. This produces an electrochemical gradient and lowers the pH within the intermembrane space. The return of the ions to their original location is used to convert the energy stored in the gradient to phosphorylate ADP to ATP. This coupled reaction is known as chemiosmotic coupling.

153. (D) Glucose is the primary product of photosynthesis and is used in the manufacture of cellulose and starch in plants and glycogen in animals. It is one of the three primary monosaccharides, along with fructose and galactose, that are most quickly absorbed during digestion. Glucose is also known historically as dextrose because of its ability to rotate light to the right (*dextro-*) when the light is passed through a solution containing it.

154. (C) Epimers are carbon-based polymers that can be differentiated not by chemical formula, meaning that they have identical atomic content, but by structure. Epimers are stereoisomers that are identical except for a single –OH reorientation, such as that seen with glucose and galactose at the C-4 position.

155. (D) An equilibrium constant is not dependent on the concentration of either the initial chemical product or the reactant, but is dependent on the reaction temperature. This constant can be derived as a reaction quotient only after the reaction reaches equilibrium, where the rate forward is the same as the reverse rate.

156. (A) The natural logarithm of the equilibrium constant (K_{eq}) is equal to the change in free energy (ΔG) divided by the molar heat capacity (R, in Joule * mol^{-1} * Kelvin^{-1}) times T (degrees Kelvin).

157. (B) Biologic monosaccharides are most commonly hexoses (with six carbon atoms) or pentoses (with five carbon atoms). Also common are disaccharides composed of two monosaccharides, whether they be pentoses or hexoses. Perhaps the most common disaccharides are sucrose (a combination of glucose and fructose) and lactose (a combination of galactose and glucose). By far the most common pentoses that are of biological importance are ribose and deoxyribose, both of which are major constituents in RNA and DNA, respectively.

158. (E) Glycogen and starch are both forms of polysaccharides. The former is highly branched and is formed in the livers of animals, while the latter is mostly unbranched and is formed in plants. While polypeptides are long, unbranched chains of amino acids, in biologic systems, they are commonly found as glycoproteins, which are polypeptides onto which sometimes numerous carbohydrate side chains have been attached.

159. (C) Acetyl-coenzyme A (or acetyl-CoA) is the end product of glycolysis and pyruvate conversion and contains two carbon atoms. These molecules are fed into the TCA cycle; this drives the cycle one complete turn, which results in the release of the these two carbon atoms as CO_2 waste gas.

160. (C) The central metabolic process most commonly known as the Krebs cycle (from its discoverer, Hans Krebs, in 1937) has also more recently been identified as the citric acid cycle (a compound containing four carbon atoms that regenerates the cycle) or the tricarboxylic acid (or TCA) cycle (because the citric acid contains three carboxyl groups).

161. (A) When a vertebrate fasts, the blood sugar level begins to drop as the animal becomes hypoglycemic. In order to correct for this event, and to maintain homeostasis, the liver becomes involved in both the breakdown of the energy storage product glycogen, which releases glucose into the bloodstream, and the synthesis of new glucose from a variety of molecular sources, including pyruvate, glycerol, and some amino acids.

162. (D) ATP is a high-energy-containing molecule that commonly acts as a coenzyme and consists of the nitrogenous base adenine coupled to the pentose ribose (forming the nucleoside adenosine). Attached to this core can commonly be found a single inorganic phosphate group (low-energy adenosine monophosphate, or AMP), two sequential phosphate groups (mid-energy-containing adenosine diphosphate, or ADP), or, ultimately, three inorganic phosphate groups in sequence (high-energy-containing adenosine triphosphate, or ATP). When energy is released from this molecule by removing the terminal electron-carrying phosphate group, the end products are ADP + Pi.

163. (A) The classical process of glycolysis starts with a single molecule of glucose, to which are then added two high-energy phosphate groups before the six-carbon glucose molecule is converted into two three-carbon molecules of pyruvate in a series of nine enzymatic steps. The intermediate fructose 1,6-biphosphate is coupled to a second phosphate group to produce fructose 1,6-biphosphate by the enzyme phosphofructokinase just prior to cleavage into two three-carbon intermediates of glycelaldehyde 3-phosphate and dihydroxyacetone phosphate.

164. (D) While the difference in the phosphate group may seem minor, the biochemical difference is massive. Only NADH is used in catabolic reactions in all cells, whereas NADPH is used only in anabolic reactions associated with photosynthesis in plants. The key is in the respective enzymes' ability to discriminate between the two.

165. (B) Any organic compound with a –COOH carboxyl group is a carboxylic acid. Any organic compound that lacks a cyclic feature such as a benzene ring is classified as aliphatic. A fatty acid may be either saturated (where each carbon atom in the chain is bonded to as many hydrogen atoms as possible) or unsaturated (where carbon-to-carbon double bonds exist).

166. (D) A flavoprotein is a protein that is conjugated to a compound derived from vitamin B_2, or riboflavin. Beside those characteristics already identified, flavoproteins are also associated with mutation repair, control of superoxide radicals, and the electron transport chain.

167. (B) Cells of multicellular organisms can cease to function and die through one of two major mechanisms: by program or by trauma. The mechanism of programmed cell death, also known as apoptosis, consists of a series of metabolic and enzymatic processes that result in the orderly breakdown and containment of cellular materials, which are then removed by phagocytosis. In contrast, cells that die as a result of external trauma produce the uncontrolled release of active cellular materials that damage adjacent cells and tissues, resulting in damaging inflammatory processes.

Chapter 5: Eukaryotic Cells

168. (B) Options A and D can both be excluded because the pressure increase seen in tube A occurred prior to the introduction of the acid and, in fact, appears to have dampened the process that was occurring before that. Option C can be excluded because respiration could not occur in tube C because of the lack of substrate. The gas is being released by the presence of something that is present in the cells themselves, here an enzyme that uses the hydrogen peroxide as a reactant.

169. (C) Option A is nonsensical. Neither option B nor option D would physically occur, and both are excluded by the control reactions in tube B. The denaturation of the enzyme peroxidase, and its removal as a catalyst, can fully account for these data.

170. (A) Tube B served as a nonbiologic control. The fact that no pressure was detected (and thus no gas production was observed) indicates that the reactions observed were organic in origin.

171. (D) The only difference between tubes A and C was the addition of a sugar substrate that would indicate the role that metabolic processes had in the gas production. However, this assay detects the processing of hydrogen peroxide into water and oxygen gas, which was the result of enzymes that had already been formed and were present in the cells when they were activated at the beginning of the exercise. While slight differences were noted, these were insignificant, eliminating the role of metabolism as the major source of gas production.

172. (A) Beta-lactamase is an enzyme produced by some bacteria as a defense against beta-lactam drugs such as penicillin. Beta-galactosidase is a component of a bacterial cell's ability to utilize lactose as a sole carbon source. Hyaluronidase is an enzyme produced by animals such as leaches as well as by some pathogenic bacteria that degrade hyaluronic acid in the general tissue matrix of animals. Both catalase and peroxidase detoxify hydrogen peroxide by converting it to water and less toxic oxygen gas.

173. (E) Of the tissues identified, cartilage is the slowest healing because the chondrocytes are bound in a tight matrix with few nutritional resources.

174. (C) Vesicles associated with cellular manufacturing are formed at regions of the ER furthest from the nucleus; they then bud off and move to the nearby Golgi apparatus, where their contents are further modified and structurally completed for their cellular function.

175. (E) Small charged ions such as Ca^{2+}, Na^+, and Cl^- cannot pass through the hydrophobic and uncharged regions in the interior of a cell membrane without a protein with a secondary structure forming a transmembrane α helix through which specific ions can flow.

176. (E) A cytoskeleton, composed of protein microfilaments, is responsible for maintaining cell structure and for providing a framework for intracellular transport. Cytoskeletons are universally found within all eukaryotic cells and have also been recently discovered in some bacteria as well.

177. (A) The fluidity of a membrane is a measure of its rigidity; the more fluid it is, the less rigid the membrane. Irregularity increases fluidity. Unsaturated fatty acids are kinked and inhibit close packing. Decreasing the lengths of these fatty acids would decrease their density, increasing fluidity.

178. (E) Connective tissue is one of the four major tissue classifications within the body and comprises about 25 percent of body mass. It includes cartilage, bone, adipose tissue, lymphatic and blood components, and collagen. The other three major types of tissue are epithelial, nervous, and muscle, confirming option E as the correct choice.

179. (E) Motions that are commonly observed and measured include movement laterally, rotation around the longitudinal axis at up to 30,000 rpm, bending of the fatty acid tail, and the much more infrequent flip-flop from one leaflet to the other. What does not occur, however, is a reversal of the hydrophilic phospholipid head from the outside of the membrane to the strongly hydrophobic middle interface between the two leaflets.

180. (A) The only gated transport of substances into the cell is through ion channels that are much too small for proteins. Substances, including ribosomal proteins and enzymes synthesized in the cytosol, are escorted into the nucleus via gated nuclear transport.

181. (D) A cytoskeleton is composed of three primary protein components: the small microfilaments (MF) of about 7 nm diameter, the larger intermediate filaments (IF) of 6–12 nm diameter, and the still larger microtubules (MT) with a diameter of 15 nm on the inside and 25 nm on the outside.

182. (D) A glucose molecule is too large to pass through a membrane without significant protein assistance. While coupled transport can be used to transport glucose, it is effective only when it is accompanied by the gradient. The loading of glucose from the intestinal lumen, where the glucose level is low, into an epithelial cell, where the level is higher, requires carrier-mediated active transport.

183. (B) A peculiarity of fatty acid synthesis is that the molecules always contain an even number of carbon atoms. The membrane diglyceride tails are 18–20 carbon atoms in length. If they were longer, then the membrane would become too inflexible and of insufficient fluidity to allow most vital nutrients to pass through.

184. (A) A special signal sequence of amino acids directs a protein being synthesized in the cytosol to attach to receptor proteins unique to the chloroplast. Once attached, the ribosome-protein-receptor assembly moves laterally along the surface of the chloroplast until it encounters a transport protein. The signal sequence and the remainder of the newly synthesized protein then pass through the opening to the interior of the chloroplast, where it begins to refold into its functioning tertiary configuration. Once this is complete and the protein is released from the ribosome, the signal sequence is removed.

185. (C) Translation always takes place in the cytosol. The resulting ribosomal proteins are then escorted back into the nucleus. Ribosomal RNA is then transcribed, where it congregates with the imported ribosomal proteins to form the ribosomal subunits.

186. (D) The sudden influx of calcium ions from the sarcolemma of muscle cells into the cytosol, which changes the actin-myosin interaction and produces the classic muscle contraction, is enabled by the much higher concentration of these ions outside the cell when compared to inside the cell. In order to precipitate sufficient ion shift, the differential has to be on the order of 10,000:1.

187. (C) The fetal gastrula differentiates into the ectoderm, endoderm, and mesoderm. The ectoderm gives rise to the epidermis and nervous system. The endoderm gives rise to glands and the lining of the lungs and gastrointestinal system. The mesoderm gives rise to the dermis, the circulatory system, the skeletal system, muscle, gonads, and the excretory system.

188. (D) Epithelial tissue serves to provide lining for organs and tissues. This includes the skin as well as organ coverings. Because they are associated with protection, the cells making up these tissues are organized and layered. While option E might seem out of place, exocrine glands are epithelial tissues and can be discarded. Complex columnar epithelium is a pure distractor and does not exist.

189. (C) Glycosylation is a process that is part of normal cellular function and is observable in proteins that are synthesized throughout the G_0 phase. The degree of glycosylation has no effect on membrane permeability, as these structures are always located on the exterior leaflet. These membrane proteins are no more or less likely to be cross-linked than any other protein.

190. (B) Often, when a new protein is synthesized into the lumen of the endoplasmic reticulum, its activity is dependent on its folding differently from its lowest-energy-requiring form. In order to overcome this issue with the second law of thermodynamics, special chaperone proteins will assist the folding.

191. (E) Microfilaments, the thinnest of the cytoskeletal framework proteins, are responsible for a number of cellular functions. These include movement within the interior of the cell, contraction of the cleavage furrow prior to the completion of cytokinesis and cellular division, cell shape, and participation in muscle cell contraction.

192. (E) The endosymbiotic theory is one that hypothesizes that the two metabolic organelles of eukaryotic cells, the chloroplast and the mitochondrion, are descendants of bacteria that began a symbiotic relationship with a primitive nucleated cell in antiquity. Lines of support, as listed in options A, B, C, and D (but not E), increase the acceptability of this theory.

193. (B) A structure described as reticular (or network) would represent a loose, not a condensed organization. The matrix supporting adipose tissue is well defined and not diffuse. While blood vessels might present on the surface as "spider veins," the interior lining is actually quite enclosed; otherwise, the blood would leak out of the capillaries and other blood vessels.

194. (B) Apoptosis is a regimented and controlled mechanism triggered by attachment of a signal protein. The cell first prepares its nuclear contents for neat destruction followed by the processing of its cytosol. When this is completed, the neatly packaged and degraded materials are easily cleaned up and disposed of by macrophages with no adjacent tissue damage.

195. (C) Because the nucleus initiates the process that ends with protein synthesis, it stays in close proximity to the endoplasmic reticulum. The DNA is anchored to the inner nuclear lamina. The passage of materials into or out of the nucleus is tightly controlled, with nuclear pores that are not simple barrel proteins, but rather are very large complexes of more than 100 components.

196. (D) The level of glucose within the intestinal epithelial cell is greater than that in both the intestinal lumen and the tissues inside the body opposite to the lumen. Because the sodium levels are much higher in the lumen than in the cell, the strong flow of Na+ into the cell is harnessed to bring in glucose as well by symport, not in the reverse direction.

197. (A) Glycolysis, the breakdown of glucose into two molecules of pyruvate, takes place within the cytosol. The high-energy electrons harvested during this process and the TCA cycle are used to reduce NAD to NADH, which then carries these to the mitochondria, where they produce 36 ATP per glucose molecule.

198. (B) Connective tissue is composed of many fibrous proteins, cells, and substances, including water, which is associated with filling spaces. Common materials included in connective tissue include the materials identified in options A, C, D, and E. While a tendon is considered a connective tissue, it is not a material that makes up connective tissue.

199. (D) Cancers are precipitated by some form of mutagenesis, followed by increased sensitivity to and production of growth factors and a loss of sensitivity to downward growth signals. The fail-safe, activation of apoptosis, is lost as well. One factor that greatly enhances tumor growth is angiogenesis, but this does not occur in all cancers.

200. (D) The number of specific organelles within a cell depends on the peculiar functions required by that cell. Cells that require high energy production and high oxygen availability, such as neurons, may well contain thousands of mitochondria in order to be sufficiently powered.

201. (B) The ER is one vast, highly convoluted structure that is continuous from the nuclear envelope to the regions adjacent to the Golgi apparatus. The RER is found closer to the nucleus and is the region where ribosomes congregate to synthesize proteins into the ER. The SER is free of simple ribosomes and is the region where protein modifications take place.

202. (B) The nucleolus, which occupies about 25 percent of the nuclear volume, is the site of the transcription of rRNA and the area of the assembly of ribosomal subunits.

203. (E) The lysosome contains more than 40 inert enzymes and compounds that become active when the lysosome fuses with a phagosome containing larger cell-sized materials, becoming a cellular version of a stomach.

204. (E) Apoptosis is programmed cell death. It can be triggered from the outside by the attachment of a signal molecule such as Fas or α-TNF to what is morbidly known as a death receptor. Alternatively, the release of cytochrome c from a damaged mitochondrion, which binds to cytosolic proteins to produce an activating apoptosome, can also initiate the process. Either activation sequence then generates a series of caspases that complete the process.

205. (A) The nucleus serves as the repository of genetic information. Signals from outside the cell generate messengers that pass into the nucleus and serve to decide what "pages" of code will be transcribed from the form of DNA into the form of RNA. These transcripts are then transferred outside the nucleus, where they are translated into the language of proteins for form and function. The concept of storing information best describes a library.

206. (A) M cells are macrophage-derived cells. What glial cells are to nervous tissue and what macrophages are to bone, cartilage, and muscle, M cells are to the small intestine.

207. (C) Small uncharged hydrophobic molecules can pass through a cell membrane unimpeded. Slightly larger uncharged polar molecules can pass through a membrane, but require regulation. Large uncharged molecules require carrier assistance to pass through the membrane. The membrane is impervious to the passage of ions, which require gated proteins to permit their passage.

208. (B) Proteins may be embedded in the membrane or simply attached to it in order to perform their function. Embedded proteins serve as carriers, as anchors for the cytoskeleton, and as receptors for cell communication molecules. The only thing that membrane-bound proteins are not associated with is storing substances, which would best be accomplished by vesicles.

Chapter 6: Viruses and Prokaryotes

209. (A) The vast majority of eubacteria have cell walls composed of peptidoglycan. These walls come in two basic types: those with a single thick layer just outside the cell membrane (identified as Gram positive), and those with a much thinner cell wall, outside of which lies a second outer membrane composed of endotoxin-containing lipids (Gram negative). Gram positive cells retain the initial primary stain of crystal violet, especially after the addition of the iodine mordant, and will appear dark blue to purple under oil immersion.

210. (D) If the iodine mordant was not added, then the crystal violet would be much more likely to be lost to the cell during the alcohol decolorization step. Even cells with thick cell walls that would normally retain the first stain and appear dark blue would improperly decolorize and appear as if they were Gram negative.

211. (A) The purpose of the alcohol step is to remove the crystal violet from all thin-walled Gram negative cells, allowing them to take on the red counterstain and appear red under the microscope. If this decolorization step was skipped, then all cells would retain the crystal violet, and all cells would appear as if they were Gram positive.

212. (B) The purpose of the heat fixation step is to ensure that all bacterial cells will adhere to the glass slide. The slides should not be overheated, as this tends to destroy the integrity of the cell walls, but too little heating, or none at all, will cause the cells to wash off the slide during the first rinse. Thus, skipping this step would mean that no cells would be observed.

213. (C) Leaving the crystal violet on the cells too long only means that the cells will stain blue. Unless the stain dries out, the alcohol will still remove this primary stain because of the thinness of the Gram negative cell wall. Thus, overstaining has no real effect on the staining process.

214. (B) The only accurate comparison between a bacterial coccus and a polyhedral virus is their general overall spherical shape.

215. (A) The flagellum is composed of three basic parts: the basal body, the hook, and the axial filament, composed of repeating flagellin subunits. The basal body rests upon the surface of the cell membrane, and the hook extends through the cell wall.

216. (C) Chitin is the polysaccharide used by fungi to construct their cell wall. Cellulose is the cell wall material used by plants, not bacteria. Lactose is a disaccharide that is not used as a cell wall component in any organism. Chromatin is a descriptive term used to describe eukaryotic DNA, not the bacterial genome. Actin is similarly not associated with the cell wall. Fungi use chitin to build their cell walls and bacteria use peptidoglycan.

217. (C) Seven genera of bacteria can form endospores. These are most analogous to lifeboats that are formed and released under hostile environments to permit the organism to survive in a highly condensed and nonmetabolizing form.

218. (B) Bacteria are much simpler in form and function compared to eukaryotes. Because of their genomic size, eukaryotic cells must separate their ability to grow and metabolize from their ability to divide into separate phases of a cell cycle. Bacteria, on the other hand, are capable of DNA replication, transcription, and translation cellular division by binary fission all at the same time.

219. (B) Viruses are organized into the seven classes of the Baltimore system. Class I includes the double-stranded DNA viruses variola, which causes smallpox, herpes viruses, adenoviruses, and the T-even bacteriophages.

220. (D) The rickettsia are bacteria and thus possess all the characteristics that define those organisms. They and the chlamydia are two bacterial groups that are obligate intracellular parasites, like all viruses.

221. (A) A back mutation restores the wild type. A second mutation that restores the original phenotype is called a suppressor mutation. A frame-shift mutation describes any mutation that adds or subtracts a base or bases within the mRNA that drastically changes the coding for the amino acids downstream from the change.

222. (A) Antibiotics usually work against bacteria by targeting some structure or mechanism that is distinctive within those cells. INH works against only a certain class of bacteria whose cell walls are composed partially of waxy mycolic acids. Only one of the three bacteria listed are within this group, the genus *Mycobacterium*, species of which cause tuberculosis and leprosy.

223. (A) A transposon is a mobile genetic element that codes only for its own reproduction. Restriction endonucleases are identified by the first letter of the genus and the first two letters of the species, such as *Eco*RI (from *Escherichia coli*). The lowercase letter "p" is commonly used to designate a plasmid.

224. (D) Replica plating involves growing colonies of suspected mutant-containing colonies on nutritionally complete media. A sterile piece of cloth is then used to transfer some of the colonies onto media that usually lack some key substrate or growth factor. Nutritionally deficient mutants can therefore be identified as those colonies that could grow on the original plate but are missing on the replicas that lacked the key component.

225. (C) Plasmids are small circular double-stranded DNA components that are self-replicating. They usually contain a number of genes that can be expressed in the bacterial cells in which they are found and are normally classified based on this transferable function.

226. (D) Viroids are segments of naked single-stranded RNA that are transferable between plants by arthropods that produce diseases in the hosts. They are not viruses because they lack envelopes and capsids. Multipartite viruses are unique to plants and have multiple genomes packaged into separate nonhelical capsids.

227. (E) Bacteria that can survive in both oxygen-rich and oxygen-deficient conditions are called facultative anaerobes. None of the gases that are most common in the atmosphere are toxic to facultative anaerobes. This includes water vapor, oxygen, carbon dioxide, and nitrogen. Only chlorine, a halogen that is toxic to all life forms because of its denaturing effect on proteins, would be hazardous to facultative anaerobes.

228. (A) Warts are the result of uncontrolled cell growth. The infectious agent that causes warts is spread by contact. Human genital warts are caused by infection of epithelial tissues with the human papillomavirus (HPV), primarily of genotypes 6/11, which is why the new HPV vaccine immunizes against these normally non-cancer-causing strains.

229. (C) Consuming a material as a sole carbon source simply means that the bacterium could survive if it were fed no organic material other than DNA, and that energy, carbon, and electrons could be derived from this source. Because DNA is degradable by many bacteria, this is not the threat it might sound like. In essence, this is no big deal.

230. (B) Transformation is the process of moving naked DNA from cell to cell. It was shown in classic experiments in the late 1920s that DNA from dead bacterial cells could be incorporated into living cells, transforming them from nonpathogenic to pathogenic forms in mice.

231. (A) The term generation time means the amount of time required for a bacterial culture in the log phase to double in number, that is, the time necessary for every cell to divide once. Knowing this, if there are 10 cells at $t = 0$ min, then there would be 20 at $t = 20$ min, 40 at $t = 40$ min, 80 at $t = 60$ min, and so on. Continuing the count brings you to a total of 5,012 at $t = 180$ min.

232. (D) When bacteria are first introduced into a fresh culture medium, they pass through the lag, log, and stationary phases. When the final depletion of nutrients is completed, the culture starts to die off, and the number of viable cells steadily drops as the culture passes through a logarithmic decline phase on its way to extinction.

233. (E) The techniques used to stain bacterial cells in order to visualize them under a light microscope are as old as the science of microbiology itself. The Gram stain is universal, as it differentiates thick-walled Gram positive cells from thin-walled Gram negative cells.

234. (A) The cell walls of the two are of different materials, with peptidoglycan being used by bacteria and chitin by fungi. The bacterial genome is organized as a single circular double-stranded DNA loop, while a fungal genome is packaged as linear chromosomes within a nucleus. Bacterial ribosomes are identified as 70S, while eukaryotic ribosomes are 80S. Bacteria are not diploid, and thus cannot reproduce with sexual mechanisms, whereas fungi, in the filamentous form, can.

235. (C) In order for a virus to replicate, it must first attach to a host cell, eliminating all choices but A and C. Once it is attached, the virus either forces the cell to bring the virus into the cytosol by endocytosis or introduces its genome by injection. This eliminates option A and makes option C the correct choice.

236. (B) The reason that bubbles form with some bacteria is that they have the enzyme peroxidase, which catalyzes the reaction that converts H_2O_2 into water and the much less toxic oxygen gas O_2 (thus the bubbles), and, because this organism can detoxify oxygen, it can grow under aerobic conditions.

237. (D) Inhalation anthrax occurs when a person inhales anthrax endospores from some source. These change from endospores to vegetative cells under the conditions found in the lungs and very rapidly grow and produce numerous toxins that characterize this fatal infection. The only way this person could be helped is to begin an immediate regimen of appropriate antibiotics.

238. (D) Ambisense viral genomes encode their proteins in two different directions, and these genes may even overlap; however, the host cell ribosome can still read the mRNA in only one direction. The reverse sequence code must be transcribed into a complementary strand that is read in the same molecular direction: 3′ to 5′.

239. (C) No matter how they are disguised, circular double-stranded DNA and 70S ribosomes indicate a bacterial cell. Option C is correct, in spite of a lack of a cell wall, because of two possibilities: the organism may be a mycoplasma or may be a penicillin-induced L-form.

240. (B) By most definitions, a virus is considered nonliving, although admittedly our definition of life is deliberately constructed to exclude viruses. The only statement that is not true of viruses is that they have a membrane. Many viruses lack a lipid envelope, and their exterior surface is composed entirely of protein.

241. (E) A prion is a protein produced by a mutated *PrP* gene that is highly resistant to degradation and that has the ability to convert the normal protein form into a mutant configuration. If a person (or animal) ingests this prion, it slowly accumulates in the nervous system and produces a spongiform encephalopathy and eventual death.

242. (E) Transduction is a technique in which DNA is packaged into lysogenic phages for transfer to other susceptible cells. It exists in two forms: transfer of specific sequences, known as specialized transduction, and transfer of random sequences, known as generalized transduction.

243. (B) Halogens are known for their affinity to attract electrons from other atoms. When halogens target atoms that are contained within organic materials, this loss of electrons can cause significant changes in their tertiary structure. This causes denaturation of proteins, loss of protein function, and eventual death of the dysfunctional cell.

244. (A) An infectious agent that presents with a complex protein is either a virus or a prion. The question provides a classic description of a complex bacteriophage such as T4.

245. (A) Horizontal transfer of DNA refers to the movement of genes from one cell to an unrelated cell, perhaps even to a different species. The horizontal transfer of resistance plasmids, with the coding for multiple drug resistance, is identified in option A.

246. (C) In order for a virus to take over a cell, it must first attach to the target cell's membrane via a very specific protein that acts as a receptor. If the cell lacks the receptor, then the cell is invulnerable to the entry of that virus. What protects us from all bacteriophages is that they target receptors that are found only on bacterial surfaces and are not found in our blood or tissues.

247. (B) An intron is not a mobile genetic element. A DNA transposon is the simplest of these elements in eukaryotes, but it has no similarity to viruses. LINE and SINE refer to Long (and Short) INterspersed Elements, respectively. These are also known as nonviral retrotransposons. This leaves option B as the correct one, which describes LTR (Long Terminal Repeats) elements that contain retroviral genes.

248. (E) Any enzyme that synthesizes DNA would be identified as a DNA polymerase. No enzyme is capable of synthesizing proteins. Nucleic acid polymerases work by synthesizing a strand that is complementary to the template, and this complementarity requires an antiparallel molecular orientation.

249. (D) The Shine-Dalgarno sequence is essential for mRNA to correctly orient alongside the 16S rRNA in the ribosome prior to translation. It is found within the nontranslated leader sequence of mRNA. This eliminates options A, B, and C from consideration, as they all refer to DNA, not RNA. This means that option D can be confirmed by elimination, even if the function of the sequence was not known.

Chapter 7: Cell Genome and Reproduction

250. (D) Ribosomes that are identified as 70S means that they are eubacterial. The lack of a cell wall in eubacteria can result from two sources. The first is the artificial removal of the cell wall by growing the cells in the presence of substances such as penicillin that interfere with cell wall formation. These cells are known as L forms. The second type lacking a cell wall includes a small group of eubacteria that naturally lack a wall, typical of the genus *Mycoplasma*.

251. (B) Molecular oxygen is toxic to obligate anaerobes because they lack the ability to detoxify the damaging gas through the presence of peroxidase of catalase enzymes. Both options A and C are eukaryotic protozoans, which normally have multiple detoxifying pathways to protect them. *Bacillus thuringensis* is protected by these pathways as well and is an aerobe. The genus *Clostridium* is a frank anaerobe, but it can survive under anaerobic conditions once it has formed resistant endospores.

252. (B) Terminal differentiation is a characteristic of multicellular eukaryotic organisms. This differentiation is triggered by the reception and binding of specific cell signals or hormones. The most characteristic of these cells are the pluripotent stem cells of the bone marrow, which can be nurtured into any of the cells found in the blood.

253. (C) The classic demonstration of bacterial transformation, or change in genetic content by the simple intake of fragments of foreign DNA into a bacterial cell, was first clearly observed in *Streptococcus pneumoniae*, which can exist as either a rough colony variant lacking a cell capsule or a smooth colony variant with a capsule. The production of the capsule is encoded within a bacterial plasmid, and the loss of the plasmid, in a process called curing, changes the phenotype from smooth to rough.

254. (A) Cells can be destroyed in two ways. The messiest way is by an uncontrolled disruption of the cell membrane. With this barrier breached, which is responsible for maintaining homeostasis, the cell cannot maintain cellular functions; the membrane dissociates, and the cytoplasmic contents leak out into the surroundings. In an animal, this elicits an inflammatory response. The alternative mechanism, called apoptosis, is much more organized and results in programmed cell death that lacks the inflammatory response. This process can be initiated by an immune cell such as a T_{CTL} cell that initiates apoptosis.

255. (A) Centrioles are on both extremes; this eliminates options C, D, and E. A centrosome is the structure that contains the centromeres. During prometaphase, special protein structures called kinetochores are assembled on the sides of the chromosomal centromeres.

256. (C) Cells communicate with one another by ligand-receptor interactions. The binding of a ligand to a membrane protein triggers conformational changes in the receptor on the cytosolic side of the membrane, which, in turn, produces second messengers that then serve to produce changes in gene expression. Antibodies can block this ligand-receptor interaction.

257. (B) The centromere is a region on a chromosome that contains a specific DNA sequence that determines the attachment point between sister chromatids. The kinetochore, located at the centromere, permits attachment of the microtubules associated with chromosomal separation during the anaphase portion of mitosis.

258. (D) *Telos* in Greek refers to the end, remoteness, or far away. *Meros*, also Greek, refers to a part or portion. Thus, *telomere* means "parts on the ends." Telomeres are the terminal repeated sequences found on the ends of chromosomes that are associated with stabilizing the ends; thus option D is correct.

259. (D) During gametogenesis, the original diploid mother cell (2n) undergoes DNA replication to become tetraploid (4n). At this point, meiosis proper begins when the chromatids align and exchange DNA segments during a process called crossing over. This cell then undergoes two consecutive reduction divisions, first becoming two diploid cells (2n) and then becoming four haploid cells (1n), completing meiosis and the formation of the gametes.

260. (B) During anaphase of mitosis, the proteins of the microtubules attach to both the chromosomal kinetochores and the spindle poles segregated at opposite ends of the dividing cell. In order for the chromosomes to move toward the poles by the functioning of molecular motors rather than the poles moving toward the chromosomes, the spindle poles must be anchored in location.

261. (A) Protein hormones bind to very specific receptor molecules expressed on the surface of cells. Once bound, they produce a second messenger, such as cAMP, that greatly amplifies the signal. Steroid hormones ignore surface receptors and pass freely through the cell membrane. Once in the cytosol, they bind to cytosolic receptors.

262. (A) Oncogenesis is the formation of a cancer. An oncogene is usually a gene that once was associated with growth regulation of a cell, but that has mutated into a form that can no longer fulfill that function. The term *proto-oncogene* is used to describe any growth-regulatory gene that has the potential to be mutated into an oncogene.

263. (B) The *Wnt* pathway has a significant role in controlling cell growth, but loss of this control resulting in a cancer is associated with mutations. HPV does interfere with p53, but in doing so, it prevents, not causes, cell death. There are more than 50 DNA repair mechanisms, none of which are affected by viral expression. The viral capsid protein identified as L1 commonly is not even expressed in cells that have been transformed into cancers by HPV.

264. (E) Prometaphase includes some of the cellular division machinery formation, some of which is normally included in late prophase and some of which is included in early metaphase. Identified with the new phase are the breakdown of the nuclear membrane, the formation of kinetochores, and the development of microtubules from the centrosomes.

265. (C) Functioning oncogenes are usually associated with controlling cell growth and reproduction. When an oncogene is mutated, or another gene that regulates the oncogene is mutated, the cell can lose the ability to control its own growth, and this process often involves the prevention of apoptosis.

266. (A) Asters, so named because of their starlike appearance under a microscope, are actually constructed of microtubules that provide the astral rays with their form. These microtubules attach to both the kinetochores on the separating chromosomes and the enveloped centrosomes that are anchored on opposite sides of the dividing cell.

267. (D) Researchers in the 1970s first found the "beads on a string" pattern associated with DNA packaging after digestion with solvents. Further analysis discovered that there were four pairs of histones (two each of H2A, H2B, H3, and H4) that served as a core or spool around which 146 nucleotide base pairs were wound. These nucleosomes are connected together in series by an additional 50 base pairs of linker DNA each.

268. (B) The σ^{70} subunit is used to identify where the RNA polymerase core enzyme components ($2\alpha + \beta + \beta'$) will bind to DNA just prior to transcription, but these are found only in prokaryotes. The eukaryotic RNA-P core enzyme components are not associated with the initial recognition of the binding site. Both transcription factor IID (TFIID) and a supporting σ-factor are required for accurate recognition.

269. (D) Histones are proteins that contain no repeating nucleic acid sequences. Nucleosomes are regions of organized DNA with any sequence structure. Simple repetitive nucleic acid sequences are found in telomeres on the ends of chromosomes; microsatellites are found throughout the genome and within the centrosome regions as well.

270. (B) mRNA produced by bacteria has a simpler structure than that of eukaryotes. Both eukaryotic and prokaryotic mRNAs have a nontranslated leader sequence that is shorter in the prokaryotic version. Bacteria have a short region where the molecule flips back on itself, forming a hairpin loop and demonstrating double-strandedness because of the complementarity regions.

271. (D) Pluripotent stem cells differ from multipotent stem cells such as those found in the bone marrow in that the latter can differentiate only into the various blood cells, whereas the former can differentiate into any cell type. Shinya Yamanaka demonstrated in 2006 that the introduction of four genes into adult differentiated cells could be used to produce induced pluripotent stem cells. For this discovery, he and John Gurdon were awarded the Nobel Prize in 2012.

272. (C) The replisome is a cluster of proteins, enzymes, and assorted cofactors that are congregated together in the nucleus after being manufactured during the G_1 phase of the cell cycle. Their function is to replicate the entire DNA genome prior to cellular division. This machinery is not associated with RNA at all. It also has nothing to do with protein synthesis.

273. (C) There are no enzymes that rejoin introns. Rejoining exons is not the function of a ribozyme. There is no enzyme that terminates translation. Any RNA that affects transcription is called RNAi, or interfering RNA, and not a ribosome. A ribozyme is an autocleaving segment of RNA.

274. (B) A recent proposal for getting around the time conundrum is that new genes arise through replisomes duplicating genes and then relocating them elsewhere in the genome. Subsequent mutations of the replicant would produce new functions, while retaining the original as a continual functional gene and maintaining the required cell functions.

275. (D) A Barr body is one of the X chromosomes in a female mammalian cell that has been inactivated by becoming permanently condensed. This mechanism is necessary in order to prevent an overexpression of the genes on the X chromosome compared to that which occurs in a male cell. This inactivation occurs just after the formation of the inner cell mass, and each cell present at that time passes on the same inactivated chromosome to its progeny. The color patchwork of the always female tortoiseshell cat provides evidence of early and random inactivation; late inactivation would produce a uniform coloration.

276. (A) Many animals can regenerate limbs or tissues, such as a starfish regenerating from a single arm or some flatworms regenerating from a single cell. It is not related to the size of the genome, as a salamander's genome is several times greater in size than a human's. Upon losing a limb, a salamander forms a specialized cell mass called a blastema that consists of dedifferentiated tissue. It appears likely that most animals, including mammals, have traded this ability for faster healing (regeneration can take months) and better cancer control.

277. (E) Many single-celled eukaryotes, notably yeasts, have closed mitosis where the nuclear envelope remains intact through the entire process and divides after the sorted chromosomes migrate to the opposite sides of the nucleus before dividing.

278. (B) Whether a cell remains quiescent during the G_0 phase of the cell cycle or starts to follow a pathway that leads to cell division depends on the summation of both inhibitory and stimulatory external signals transduced through the cell membrane. If the signals are correct, the cell passes through the G_1 restriction checkpoint and becomes irreversibly committed to cell division. This process is activated by the interaction of protein cyclins and cyclin-dependent kinases (CDK) and commits the cell to enter the S phase.

279. (A) All cells within a body contain identical copies of that individual's unique genome, with the sole exception of lymphocytes committed to antigen specificity. However, the expression of the various genes in that genome are controlled by transcription factors, and the presence of these transcription factors is most commonly controlled by external signals from cells that are either adjacent to them or in close proximity. These signals may be received either through mechanical contact, from diffused molecules, or through gap junctions. These signals shift the recipient's cellular determination and initiate separate differentiation.

280. (E) Specific gene segments governing the structure of the variable portion of both antibodies produced by B cells and the equivalent portions of T-cell receptors undergo random gene deletion and splicing during maturation in the bone marrow and thymus, respectively. These rearrangements are expressed on the cell surface, and, if they fail to be identified as self, or if they react to and bind self-antigens, they are stimulated to undergo apoptosis.

281. (C) Spacer DNA accounts for about 24 percent of the human genome and is noncoding. Since it is noncoding, even a large deletion mutation would have no effect on gene expression or control. A mutation as described would have no effect on any gene expression.

282. (B) The lowest level of organizing eukaryotic DNA occurs when about 200 base pairs are wound around eight molecules of histones into a 10-nm structure known as a nucleosome. Successive nucleosomes are then organized into a 30-nm structure known as a chromatin fiber. Sections of chromatin fiber aggregate as heterochromatin and the DNA reaches maximum compaction in the form of the highly condensed chromosome.

283. (C) The mRNA produced by eukaryotic cells contains the code from only one gene and is always monocistronic. Cells are capable of producing two versions of a final mRNA, usually one longer version that results in a membrane-bound protein and an alternately spliced shorter version that will be secreted from the cell.

284. (E) The reproduction of mitochondria and chloroplasts is independent of the cell cycle involving nuclear replication and subsequent cell division. Both of these organelles have their own DNA, which replicates continually in a prokaryotic fashion while the cell is quiescent during interphase.

285. (A) Cellular senescence is thought to be linked to both decreased telomerase expression, which maintains telomere length and retards the toxic effects of aberrant alternate RNA splicing, and asymmetric segregation of damaged molecules and organelles during cellular division, where one daughter cell remains pristine and the other receives the bulk of the senescent materials. By eliminating this latter process, the accumulated damage would persist, and the result would be increased cancer rates.

286. (D) During embryogenesis, many cells undergo migration through the developing molecular scaffolding. When doing so, these migrating cells demonstrate polarized cell movement in response to chemical stimuli and the formation of filopodia and lamellapodia under control of the cytoskeleton, much as is seen in amoeboid chemotaxis.

287. (B) The protein produced by the p53 gene is essential for the arrest of cellular division and serves to stop the cell cycle in the G_0 phase. It thus has a role not only in controlling cellular division during development, but also in preventing the uncontrolled growth of cancer cells. Most transformed cell lines, which cause cancers in vivo, either have mutated and nonfunctional p53 protein or have a protein that interferes with p53 function.

288. (D) When a cell is in the G_0 phase, a normal nucleus consists of a full set of chromosomes from the father and a full set from the mother; thus, the cell is diploid. The matching-sized chromosomes are thus homologous. Only when the cell prepares for cellular division during the S phase does this change, when each chromosome is duplicated. The identical copies of each chromosome are sister chromatids.

289. (A) The purpose of mitosis is cellular division with the result of producing two genetically identical daughter cells. The purpose of meiosis is to produce genetically unique gametes using an additional reduction division without additional DNA replication. However, the original chromosomal replication of both processes is identical.

290. (C) Cells found within the blood are all derived from multipotent stem cells residing in the bone marrow. During cell development, a recently divided stem cell will, under guidance provided by the surrounding chemical and cellular environment, begin the differentiation process. Depending on the external stimulus, this process will proceed down different pathways, finally resulting in the release of a mature effector cell. Platelets, also known as thrombocytes, are the final differentiated form derived from the progenitor megakaryocyte.

291. (B) If a cell becomes isolated from others, this may trigger apoptosis so as to prevent the cell from growing in the wrong place. This can be seen in cell cultures when cells are plated at too low a density. Both NK cells and cytotoxic T-cell lymphocytes (T_{CTL}) search and destroy cells that have inappropriate cell markers. During the cell cycle, cells must pass through certain checkpoints and receive a "go" (survival) signal to proceed; otherwise, they undergo programmed cell death as a fail-safe mechanism. Starvation will cause death by lysis because of a failure to maintain homeostasis.

Chapter 8: Cellular Communications

292. (A) Theodore Schwann's studies in the mid-nineteenth century identified cells that surround neurons in certain nervous tissues. These cells were later identified as being important in the production of the myelin sheath that improves nerve action potential transmission. These cells are now identified as Schwann cells.

293. (D) Neurotransmitters are chemicals that brain cells and other nervous tissues use to communicate with one another. These neurotransmitters have no effect on a cell unless the receiving cell has a receptor specific for that neurotransmitter. Acetylcholine is the neurotransmitter that is most commonly used to signal a muscle to contract.

294. (B) Ion channels at the location of a neuron stimulus open, allowing a flood of sodium ions into the cell. The flood of sodium into the cell changes the resting potential charge polarity on the membrane, reversing it from −70 mV to +30 mV. As the depolarization spreads out from the original source, the initial gates close and sodium-potassium pumps rapidly restore the sodium imbalance of the action potential back to the −70 mV state.

295. (C) A neuron consists of the cell body, numerous projections from the cell body called dendrites, and a single long axon. The nucleus resides in the major portion of the cell, the cell body.

296. (B) The basic cell of the nervous system is the neuron. This eliminates option A as an incorrect choice. The axons of nerve cells, not the entire cell, are covered in myelin, eliminating option E as well. A nerve is a cluster of long axons, eliminating options C and D and making option B the best description of a nerve.

297. (D) An axon is the lengthy extension of a neuron and serves as a conduit for signal propagation. The threshold for generating an action potential is established either within dendritic connections to other nerve cells or by other cell dendritic connections to the cell body.

298. (A) Nerve impulses are sent down the axon in the form of an action potential. However, if the surface is covered with insulating myelin, then the action potential leaps from node to node in a much more rapid and energy-efficient manner, because only the gaps in insulation at the nodes are subject to the polarization-depolarization cycle.

299. (D) An inactive neuron has a resting potential of −70 mV. When the cell receives a signal, the ligand attaches at a receptor, which then opens a ligand-gated channel. The influx of ions, sodium in this case, then causes adjacent voltage-gated channel proteins to open, increasing the sodium influx. This influx causes the local charge differential to switch from −70 mV to +30 mV and is known as the depolarization phase.

300. (C) Neurotransmitters are chemicals that will activate ligand-gated channels in cells on the postsynaptic side of a synapse. Acetylcholine predominates in the neuromuscular junction. Norepinephrine is found in both the central and peripheral nervous systems. Serotonin and amino acids, which include GABA, are found only in the brain.

301. (C) Ion channels are proteins that permit the passage of specific ions through a membrane, always in the direction of a gradient. These channels are gated, meaning that they can be either open or closed. In neurons, the action potential is propagated down the neuron by the actions of voltage-gated channel proteins.

302. (D) In order for the muscle to relax following contraction, the bound neurotransmitter acetylcholine is broken down by acetylcholinesterase and recycled back to the neuron.

Nerve agents are cholinesterase inhibiters that prevent the enzyme from breaking down the bound neurotransmitter.

303. (B) Both Schwann cells and oligodendrocytes are associated with the production of the myelin sheath surrounding neuron axons, but the former are found only in the peripheral nervous system. The presence of oligodendrocytes is what results in "white matter."

304. (A) An inhibitory neuron will produce a dampening effect to prevent the formation of an action potential in an adjacent neuron. One of the best ways to counteract a buildup of positive charges in a cell as a result of a signal from a stimulatory neuron is to produce a concomitant influx of negative charges, such as Cl^- ions. Thus, when a cell receives both balanced stimulatory and inhibitory signals, the net result is no action within the receiving cell.

305. (D) Glial cells, found in the brain, are responsible for nutritional and structural support and protection of neurons in the white matter.

306. (D) The hypothalamus passes neural signals to the pituitary gland, which, in turn, secretes hormones that affect the body as a whole, including the hypothalamus.

307. (B) The nervous system is divided into two broad sections: the central nervous system (CNS) and the peripheral nervous system (PNS). The nerves within the vertebrae, known as the spinal cord, are part of the CNS, which also includes the brain and the medulla oblongata, or brain stem.

308. (C) The myelin sheath provides insulation and increases the speed of the movement of the action potential down an axon. Additionally, when the neuron is damaged, the sheath assists in its repair.

309. (A) The action potential travels down a noninsulated axon as a charge-gated ion channel opens and closes rapidly in response to the flood of ions along its length. Since ion flow across the axon membrane is impeded by the myelin sheath, there is no need to have ion channels anywhere other than at the nodes.

310. (C) When blood calcium levels drop, the parathyroid glands release parathyroid hormone (PTH), which stimulates osteoclasts in the bone to release calcium, causes the kidneys to reabsorb more calcium, and increases calcium absorption in the intestinal tract.

311. (E) Type II, or adult-onset, diabetes is frequently attributed to a loss of insulin sensitivity or excessive absorption by adipose tissue in obese individuals, but Type I, or juvenile-onset, diabetes is not. In this latter condition, the β cells of the pancreas are incapable of secreting insulin.

312. (E) When the body is under stress, the hypothalamus secretes corticotropin-releasing hormone (CRH), which stimulates the anterior pituitary to release adrenocorticotropic hormone (ACTH). ACTH, in turn, signals the adrenals to produce corticosteroids such as cortisol (or hydrocortisone), synthesized from cholesterol, which serve to increase blood sugar levels and energy-releasing metabolism.

313. (D) When a neuron receives an appropriate stimulus in the form of a neurotransmitter or mechanically gated signal, there is a sudden influx of sodium ions (Na^+). This eliminates options A, C, and E. Sodium-potassium pumps restore the original resting potential by bringing the leaked sodium back out and the escaped potassium back in.

314. (C) Every time a neuron conducts an action potential along its axon, the sodium and potassium balance of the resting potential must be restored in order for the cell to be able to send another signal; this requires huge quantities of ATP to power the sodium-potassium pumps. For this reason, neurons contain thousands of energy-generating mitochondria, which, in turn, require huge quantities of oxygen and glucose.

315. (A) The anterior pituitary releases thyroid-stimulating hormone (TSH), which stimulates the thyroid to release triiodothyronine and thyroxine (or T_3 and T_4, respectively), which, in turn, increases metabolic output and protein synthesis.

316. (D) The fight-or-flight response prepares the body for immediate action by constricting blood vessels and increasing the heart rate, thus raising blood pressure and blood output. Epinephrine and norepinephrine, released by the adrenal glands, produce the effects that can help the body survive crisis conditions.

317. (B) Nonsteroidal, or protein, hormones bind to receptors on the cell surface if they are present. This ligand-receptor interaction induces a conformational change in the receptor that modifies the cytosolic structure. This change produces a second messenger, such as cyclic AMP (cAMP), which then causes the production of a DNA-binding protein that changes genetic expression.

318. (A) In reference to the brain, a ventricle is a space that contains cerebrospinal fluid (CSF), which is essential for cushioning the brain from trauma, but which is not associated with the meninges aside from its protective function. The arachnoid and dura mater are layers of the meninges, but sulcus refers to a depression or fissure of the brain surface.

319. (D) The spinal cord is divided into five regions, all of which are associated with the control of everything below the head, and the nervous system generally descends downward from the spine. The vagus nerve, which stimulates the viscera, is included as one of the cranial nerves originating from the brain stem.

320. (E) Oxytocin, which is responsible for cervical dilation during childbirth and for feelings of contentment and fulfillment leading to bonding afterwards, and antidiuretic hormone (ADH, also known as vasopressin), which regulates fluid balance throughout the body, are both synthesized within the hypothalamus, but are stored and released by the posterior pituitary as necessary.

321. (B) Aldosterone, after its production in the adrenal cortex, increases sodium reabsorption in the kidneys while simultaneously decreasing the reabsorption of potassium. This rise in sodium ion concentration increases water retention and thus blood volume, which also increases blood pressure.

322. (A) Iodine is an essential element that is normally acquired from seafood or iodized salt. When ingested, it is transferred to the thymus, where it is incorporated into both triiodothyronine (T_3) and thyroxine (T_4). These hormones increase growth, development, and metabolism. When iodine uptake is insufficient, the thyroid attempts to compensate by enlarging in size, which produces a goiter.

323. (B) Glial cells provide both immune surveillance and production of the myelin sheath. The subarachnoid space is filled with cerebrospinal fluid (CSF). The two hemispheres of the brain are connected by the corpus callosum, which is a fluid-filled ventricle in the central portion of the brain. This plexus is responsible for production of the cushioning CSF that fills the ventricles and spaces surrounding the brain.

324. (C) Gamma-aminobutyric acid (GABA or γ-aminobutyric acid) is a neurotransmitter that causes the opening of chlorine ion channels, producing a flood of negative charges into the cell that negates the signal threshold produced by a stimulatory influx of sodium ions. As such, it serves to inhibit signal transduction and has a role in reducing the perception of pain.

325. (D) Both the thyroid and the adrenals are controlled by the anterior pituitary, but antidiuretic hormone (ADH) and oxytocin are produced by the posterior pituitary. These glands are all controlled by one other: the hypothalamus.

326. (A) The autonomic nervous system (ANS) is composed of two branches: the sympathetic nervous system and the counterbalancing parasympathetic system. Although these two work together to provide consistent functioning of the body as a whole, they are not anatomical mirror images of each other. So, even though the cranial nerves stimulate the digestion processes of the viscera, their counterparts in function are the thoracic nerves.

327. (C) There are two basic types of hormones: steroid and protein. While a steroidal hormone will pass through a cell membrane, its effect on the cell will be at the nuclear transcription level after it has bound to an appropriate receptor.

328. (B) During neurological development in fetal development, the brain initially forms three parts, roughly the fore-, mid- and hindbrain. Later differentiation of the forebrain produces the recognizable structures of the thalamus, hypothalamus, and cerebrum as well as others. The cerebrum encloses the interior lining structure of the limbic system.

329. (E) The period of rapid eye movement (REM) is controlled directly by brain function. REM is a stage of sleep that occupies about 25 percent of human sleeping time.

330. (E) Long-term stress keeps the body in a state of perpetual charge that produces damage if it is unrelieved. This includes damage to organs because of elevated blood pressure, ion imbalance and adrenal exhaustion because of the overactivity of the hormone-producing cells of the cortex and medulla, and a depletion of energy reserves because of excessive metabolic output.

331. (E) Alcohol may give the appearance of being a CNS stimulant because of the commonly observed increase in erratic behavior, but its effect is actually as a depressant of behavioral inhibitions. When consumed in excessive quantities, it suppresses brain and other functions to the point of inducing coma and death.

332. (D) Suckling produces a very comforting feeling in the mother, and thus is not associated with stress or related signals that produce adrenocorticotropic hormone or human growth hormone (HGH). Oxytocin produces a tremendous sense of well-being and contentment that increases the bonding experience.

Chapter 9: Internal Movement and Defense

333. (D) The cause of CJD and its variants found in animal nerve tissue, such as causative agents of elk wasting disease, kuru, and mad cow disease, is known as prions. Prions are actually infectious proteins that are produced either naturally in animals with mutated prion-related protein genes (PrP) or by contact with proteins produced by mutated genes. Thus, option D is the only reasonable choice.

334. (A) The chances of the same disease being inherited by four separate individuals with different backgrounds but with a common point of contact is extremely remote. Thus, option A is most reasonable.

335. (D) A cell that produces PrP, in this case neurons, usually produces the normal form, which is readily recycled and remade on a continual basis. The abnormal form, however, appears to polymerize with the normal form when making contact, producing larger and larger clusters of nondegradable protein. This progressive buildup is what produces the plaques and the pathology.

336. (C) The mutant PrP is already denatured to its least energy-containing state. As such, it is very difficult to degrade any further. The protein is resistant to further denaturation by both strong acids and autoclaving. Incineration is the best way to destroy this abnormal protein.

337. (B) In essence, the bad protein recruits normal proteins to accumulate into nondegradable clusters. These clusters then interfere with normal neuron signal transduction.

338. (D) The first thing that the body does when a deep enough breach is produced in the skin is the formation of a blood clot. Inflammatory cells then respond quickly. Fibroblasts then begin to proliferate to replace damaged cells, and macrophages will enter the wound to clear away debris. Eventually the original structure is restored by regenerating columnar cells.

339. (A) Arrector pili are smooth muscle cells that serve to pull the hairs upright so that they are perpendicular to the skin surface. This reduces airflow across the skin surface and helps the body conserve heat.

340. (B) Skin mechanoreceptors that sense touch, vibrations, or pressure include Merkel's disks, which are used to detect touch and pressure; Pacinian corpuscles, which provide data on rapid vibrations and pressure; and Meissner's corpuscles, which detect texture and vibrations. However, in this last case, these are not associated with hair follicles.

341. (C) Fingernails and toenails are composed of the same material as the outer layers of the epithelium, not of polysaccharides and not of sebum. In fact, nails not only are composed of the same material as the epithelium, keratin, but are also constructed by the same cells.

342. (A) The skin is involved in vitamin D synthesis when it is exposed to ultraviolet light. This vitamin D is then transported to the liver, where it is converted to calcidiol (and then into calcitriol in the kidneys), which helps regulate blood calcium levels and increases the absorption of calcium in the small intestine.

343. (C) The immune system is composed of primary and secondary lymphoid organs. The thymus (a primary organ) and the spleen (a secondary organ) are the organs that are the largest of the group. Lymph nodes are the next smaller in size and are more complex and organized than the other two. Of the remaining two, lymph nodules are collections of lymph follicles.

344. (D) As arterial vessels get farther from the heart, they get smaller, becoming arterioles and then tissue capillaries. As the blood returns to the heart, it flows through first venules and then veins before passing through the vena cava back into the heart.

345. (B) Neither erythrocytes nor lymphocytes are phagocytic. The three remaining choices are, but eosinophils are only slightly so, and they are few in number. While macrophages are larger than neutrophils and are each capable of phagocytosing more per cell, they are outnumbered by neutrophils by more than 3:1.

346. (E) If blood is withdrawn from the body, it immediately begins to clot. The straw-colored liquid that remains is called serum. However, if the blood is drawn into a tube containing an anticoagulant, the clotting proteins remain in the fluid phase. After the cells settle, the straw-colored liquid that remains is called plasma. Serum is plasma with the clotting proteins removed.

347. (A) Immunoglobulin is another name for an antibody. Once these glycoproteins are synthesized in lymph tissues, they circulate first through the lymph, then through the blood. While they are composed of four protein chains, these are identified as two light chains and two heavy chains bound together by disulfide bridges.

348. (A) The immune system is divided into primary and secondary lymphoid organs or tissues. The primary organs are responsible for generating and screening the cells of the immune system. The organs responsible for initially manufacturing these cells are the thymus and the bone marrow.

349. (D) Blood enters the right side of the heart at the upper chamber, the right atrium. It then passes into the lower chamber, the right ventricle. From the right ventricle, it flows through the lungs and becomes oxygenated, returning to the left atrium. It then passes from there to the left ventricle, where it is then pumped out to the body.

350. (C) Vessels that carry blood from the heart are arteries. Vessels that return blood to the heart are veins. The blood that leaves the right ventricle goes to the lungs with very little oxygen remaining. The vessels that carry it are known as the pulmonary arteries. After the blood becomes as oxygenated as it possibly can, it leaves the lungs to return to the heart through the pulmonary veins.

351. (C) When a cell becomes cancerous, it usually starts to express proteins that are normally not expressed by normal cells, and these can stimulate a specific immune response. The effector cells that attack cancer cells by inducing apoptosis are known as cytotoxic T-lymphocytes, or T_{CTL} cells.

352. (B) The only thing listed that the lymph does not do is to produce antibodies, as that is done by B-cells and plasma cells congregated in the lymphoid tissues that they pass through.

353. (E) Macrophages flowing through the blood bounce into ligands and begin to marginate, first slowly as a rolling adhesion, then with the cells becoming more firmly attached by tighter binding with additional molecules. Once they are stopped, the cells enter the tissues by going between adjacent endothelial cells (diapedesis). Once there, they migrate through the tissues toward the infected area following a signal gradient.

354. (E) Bone marrow stem cells initially differentiate into myeloid and lymphoid progenitor cells. Erythroid progenitor cells then degenerate into erythrocytes (or red blood cells).

355. (A) When a foreign antigen binds to the surface-bound antibody, it activates the B-cell response. First, the cell undergoes lymphoproliferation, producing a clone of cells, all producing the same antibody. Second, these cells all shift to manufacturing secreted antibodies. Some of these cells become memory cells, and the remainder of the activated cells will differentiate into antibody factories known as plasma cells.

356. (A) The muscle tissue of the heart is known as myocardium. Layers of epithelial tissues line this muscle on the inside (endocardium) and the outside (epicardium). However, to ensure the heart's detachment and independence from the rest of the components of the thoracic cavity, there is a sac filled with lubricating fluid surrounding the heart that is known as the pericardial cavity. Lining this sac on the outside is the pericardium.

357. (D) On the right side, the valve between the atrium and the ventricle is known as the tricuspid valve, and the valve that is between the ventricle and the pulmonary arteries is known as the pulmonary (or pulmonary semilunar) valve. Upon the blood's reentry into the heart on the left side, the valve between the atrium and the ventricle is the mitral (or bicuspid) valve, and the last in sequence, as the blood leaves the heart through the aorta, is the aortic (or aortic semilunar) valve.

358. (E) SRS-A (slow-reacting substance of anaphylaxis) does produce a systemic response, but, as its name implies, it does so slowly and causes sustained broncoconstriction. Histamine, on the other hand, produces all of the effects listed.

359. (B) Systole, when the blood pressure is at its highest, occurs when both ventricles are contracting with coordinated force, pushing blood out of the heart into the lungs and tissues simultaneously. Diastole occurs when the blood is not being pressurized by the heart.

360. (C) Cells differentiate early during hematopoiesis in the bone marrow into myeloid and lymphoid cell lines. The best choice is option C because a monocyte in the blood becomes a macrophage when it enters the tissues.

361. (A) Cells from a person with sickle cell anemia will fold in half due to a mutation in the hemoglobin protein when the cells are not saturated with oxygen, such as might occur following some physical exertion.

362. (E) An autoimmune disorder occurs when one's immune system attacks one's own body and produces damage. Type II diabetes can be caused by several things, including loss of sensitivity to insulin or its insufficient production, but none are classed as autoimmunity.

363. (C) Platelets, also known as thrombocytes because of their role in forming a thrombus (blood clot), are degenerate cell fragments found throughout the blood. Heparin is an anti-coagulant whose presence leads to the inactivation of thrombin, thus preventing effective clot formation.

364. (D) Hematopoiesis is the process of making blood, specifically the cellular components. Other than the red blood cells, all of these cells are leukocytes associated with some aspect of body defense. The thymus is a primary lymphoid organ, but the T-cells that are there migrated there during gestation from the actual site of hematopoiesis, the bone marrow.

365. (A) During hematopoiesis, progenitor lymphocytes undergo random gene rearrangements. This randomly rearranged DNA then codes for the receptor that determines the antigen specificity for that individual cell, which will be different from that for every other cell.

366. (C) The lymph system has no pump, and lymph moves slowly from the tissues through the ducts, passing through lymph nodules and nodes that provide immune surveillance by constantly searching for foreign proteins draining from the tissues. This fluid reenters the circulatory system when the lymph fluid is dumped back into the circulatory system at the vena cava.

367. (B) The sinoatrial (SA) node acts as the pacemaker of the heart. The electrical signal generated there passes through the atrioventricular (AV) node, where the heart rate is coordinated and distributed. The signal is then passed through the bundle of His (also known as the AV bundle) through the Purkinje fibers, where the nerves distribute the signals to the muscle tissue.

368. (B) The heart is one of the major consumers of both oxygen and glucose because of the huge energy expense required for constant repetitive muscle contraction. The blood providing the essential materials for its function is skimmed right off the top through the coronary arteries as it exits the heart through the ascending aorta.

369. (E) The primary antibody type in respiratory and intestinal secretions is manufactured just inside the epithelial layer of these tissues. These are then attached to a special protein called a secretory component that escorts these IgA antibodies through the epithelial cells and into the mucus, where they neutralize invaders before they have a chance to get inside the body.

370. (D) As people age, their tissues lose flexibility, including the cells that line all blood vessels, decreasing the body's ability to regulate blood pressure properly. Elevated high-density lipoprotein (HDL) levels are associated with improved cardiovascular health and improved blood pressure control.

371. (C) The primary immune response occurs following a first-time exposure to an antigen and is characterized by low levels of IgM production. The secondary response is characterized by a higher production of IgG and the subsequent production of memory cells. What doesn't seem to matter is the specific antigen; only the level and duration of exposure determines which response will be observed.

372. (E) Normally, basophils are observed at the lowest levels, with about 1 percent or less of all leukocytes. Second fewest are the eosinophils, at roughly 3 percent. Monocytes normally come in at about 10 percent, and lymphocytes at about 25 percent. Neutrophils account for the remainder of the leukocytes in circulation.

373. (A) Blood clot formation is produced by the conversion of two major factors that are present in the blood in inactive form. These factors are prothrombin and fibrinogen. In essence, inactive prothrombin becomes active thrombin, and active thrombin serves to convert inactive fibrinogen into active fibrin. Fibrin then begins to form cross-links and produces an expanding clot.

Chapter 10: Interactions with the Environment

374. (A) Several environmental variations are being evaluated: moisture versus dryness, light versus dark, and preference for or against mild acid conditions. The best single control is to observe the animals' preference for one side or the other under the same conditions, here the first half of the first run. No preference was observed, eliminating a variable based solely on which corral they are in.

375. (D) The second run provides the data for this question. During the first 5 minutes, when given the choice of a dry or a moist environment, they clearly preferred the moist. However, when the dry corral was made dark, it neutralized their preference for moisture, indicating that they equally preferred the two corrals. This is to be expected because they are terrestrial crustaceans that respire through gills and normally live under leaf litter.

376. (B) The third run provided data for the animals' preference for or against the acid environment. The preference numbers were essentially the same under both conditions, indicating that they were unaffected by the acid and had no preference.

377. (C) In order to answer this question, the conditions must be the same. This occurs only under the dry conditions during the first run. Thus, option C is the best choice.

378. (A) Although this was not directly tested, one would expect that they would have a clear preference for moist and dark conditions. This is reasonable because this is typical of their normal habitat.

379. (C) The gallbladder is an organ that stores and concentrates the bile that is produced by the liver. Bile contains numerous enzymes associated with increasing the breakdown of nutrients, such as starch, fats, nucleic acids, and proteins. What bile does not contain, however, is a cellular enzyme used for the metabolism of monosaccharides.

380. (B) Renal failure means that the kidneys are not functioning properly. Since the kidneys are responsible for the removal of nitrogenous wastes, their failure would result in a buildup of these materials in the blood, a condition known as uremia. Since fluid balance is upset by kidney failure, what commonly occurs is excess fluid retention, which causes swelling of the tissues and is seen as generalized edema (swelling).

381. (E) The colon begins at the ileocecal valve, where the large and small intestines connect. The first portion of the colon, the cecum, connects to the appendix and leads to the ascending colon, which leads to the transverse colon and then the descending colon. The descending colon connects to the rectum via the sigmoid colon, or flexure.

382. (D) In order for vitamin B_{12} to be properly absorbed, it must first be released from food in the duodenum and combined with intrinsic factor, which is produced in the stomach. This complex then moves through almost the entirety of the small intestine until it nearly reaches the juncture between the ileum and the cecum, where it is absorbed into the circulatory system.

383. (C) On a gross scale, the kidney is composed of the outer cortex, the middle medulla, and the inner pelvis. While the reabsorption tubules are what constitute most of the medulla, the filtration portions of the nephron are also located in the cortex.

384. (D) The liver synthesizes bile and enzymes associated with digestion, produces vital blood proteins, and stores more than 50 percent of the body's supply of vitamin B_{12} and iron. Blood, filled with substances absorbed in the small intestines, first passes through the liver before entering the general circulation. The liver participates in metabolism by the production of glucose from glycogen and assists in lipid metabolism.

385. (B) The gallbladder is a storage organ connected to the liver, which synthesizes the digestion-aiding gall, and the duodenum, where the gall is released after lipids are detected exiting the stomach. Since the flow of material is one way, from liver to gallbladder to duodenum, when a gallstone is passed, it can go only into the duodenum.

386. (D) Amylase is an enzyme that breaks down amylose, also known as starch, into smaller sugars and monosaccharides, primarily glucose. Digestive materials such as enzymes are produced within glands such as those found in the mouth and the liver, with enzymes being stored in the gallbladder for release into the duodenum.

387. (A) Once material passes from the blood, it is collected as a filtrate within the Bowman's capsule. This filtrate passes through the proximal tubule, down the descending tubule, around the loop of Henle, and back up through the ascending tubule. The newly formed urine is then routed out of the nephron through the distal tubule into the collecting duct.

388. (B) Hydrochloric acid is secreted in the stomach, not the liver. Glycogen is stored in the liver, where it can be broken down into glucose and released into the blood, not the bile. Nitrogenous wastes are removed in the kidneys and disposed of in the urine.

389. (C) Parietal cells produce intrinsic factor and HCl. Intrinsic factor is required for the absorption of vitamin B_{12} in the ileum of the small intestine. HCl denatures proteins, and by doing so also kills most of the microorganisms ingested with our food. HCl also converts the inactive pepsinogen into active pepsin. Mucus is produced by neck cells within the gastric pits.

390. (E) The saliva is produced by three, not four, pairs of glands. The pharyngeal tonsils, also known as adenoids, while located in the same general area as the glands responsible for saliva, are a part of the immune system and are responsible for immune surveillance of the oropharyngeal mucosa.

391. (C) The mechanism identified in the question is used to describe ion flow and the control of urine concentration.

392. (B) Proteins and blood cells never pass through the glomerular filter and stay in the blood. About 99 percent of the water is recovered. Glucose, amino acids, and carbonate are all 100 percent recovered within the proximal convoluted tubule (PCT). Both sodium and chlorine ions are recovered in the ascending tubule with about 65 percent efficiency.

393. (E) The primary function of the small intestine is to extract and absorb as many nutrients as possible from the food. The small intestine is composed of three sections in order from the stomach: duodenum, jejunum, and ileum. Digestion starts as soon as the food enters the first of these sections.

394. (B) The retention or shedding of water in the urine is controlled by antidiuretic hormone (ADH), secreted by the adrenals. When the body becomes dehydrated, then ADH is secreted to retain more water, which increases the waste concentration in the urine. Ethyl alcohol interferes with the function of ADH, thereby increasing urinary output in spite of the dehydration condition.

395. (B) Increasing water intake increases fluid levels within the blood. This, in turn, decreases ion concentration. When low ion concentrations are detected by the hypothalamus, it signals the pituitary to signal the adrenals to reduce their output of ADH, thereby increasing urinary output and restoring fluid balance.

396. (D) The sugar levels are highest in the epithelial cells and lower in both the intestinal lumen and the capillaries. Sugars within the intestinal lumen are at low levels and are valuable enough that the epithelial cells are willing to expend energy to import them by active transport. Because of the size of the molecules, they are moved into the tissues by passive carrier mediation, and then into the capillaries by simple diffusion.

397. (E) Lipid droplets are first emulsified by bile salts in the duodenum. These smaller droplets can then be penetrated by the lipases from the pancreatic juices and broken down primarily into triglycerides. These triglycerides are then packaged with proteins to form chylomicrons, which are then transported to the lymph by epithelial cells.

398. (D) The only thing listed that the kidneys are not responsible for is the disposal of bilirubin from the breakdown of hemoglobin from recycled red blood cells, which is disposed of in the bile and then dumped into the feces.

399. (B) Interspersed across the alveolar surface are septal cells that secrete surfactants. These substances are necessary in the extremely small aveolar sacs because the water protecting the cell surfaces from dehydration would cause the collapse of these sacs as a result of the cohesive power of the water. Surfactants reduce this effect and permit the alveoli to remain inflated.

400. (A) Since the last stop for inspired air is within the alveoli just before the oxygen enters the blood supply, they must be in the last position in the sequence. Similarly, the first structure encountered as air enters the respiratory system is the pharynx. The larynx is superior to the trachea, which eliminates option C and confirms option A as the correct sequence.

401. (C) When a person is at rest, the amount of air in the lungs is called the resting tidal volume (TV). If as much air as possible is forced out by the muscles, the quantity leaving is called the expiratory reserve volume (ERV). The amount of air remaining in the lungs after expelling the ERV is called the residual volume. The inspiratory reserve volume (IRV) is the measurement of the maximum amount a person can inhale.

402. (C) If you close your mouth and nose and attempt to expand your chest using the intercostal muscles, the expanded volume without an increase in air content causes a reduction in the pressure in the lungs. That reduced pressure is inversely proportional to the expanded volume. It is this reduced pressure in the lungs that allows the air to flow from the atmosphere into the alveoli. This is Boyle's law.

403. (E) If the respiratory tubes were not reinforced with inflexible material such as thick fibrous material and cartilage, they would collapse when the pressure dropped and balloon when the pressure rose. The greatest pressure changes occur in the upper regions, where the greatest pressure variations occur. This means that the pharynx, trachea, and bronchi all contain cartilage and the very small bronchioles do not.

404. (B) The cerebellum, the regulator of many involuntary activities, mostly controls coordination and body motion. The medulla oblongata helps control breathing.

405. (A) CO_2 is present at a higher concentration in the tissues than in the blood, so it enters the blood by passive diffusion. There 7 percent of it enters and remains in the blood plasma. The remaining 93 percent enters into the red blood cells: about 25 percent binds to hemoglobin, and the remaining 70 percent is converted to carbonic acid (H_2CO_3) by the enzyme carbonic anhydrase.

406. (E) Pneumonia is a condition that is defined as a fluid infiltration into the alveoli that interferes with gas exchange. The most common cause of pneumonia is bacteria. Fluid infiltration can also be caused by some types of chemical damage. Emphysema is a condition in which the alveoli lose their structural integrity. While breathing can be impaired by lung cancer, this is normally caused by a loss of access to the alveoli by blockages.

407. (A) Nitrogen is not biologically available as an atmospheric gas, which means that, to us, it is inert. This means that it moves freely into our blood and tissues until it reaches equilibrium with the atmosphere.

408. (A) Cells that line the respiratory passages have cilia that beat constantly to move this material along, both to keep the passages clean and to keep mucus from accumulating in the lungs. The goal is to get the stuff into position either for being removed from the body by expectoration (spitting) or for being swallowed and destroyed in the acid environment of the stomach.

409. (E) There are two lungs in the human thoracic cavity, one on the right side of the heart and one on the left. The right lung is composed of three separate lobes, and the left is composed of two. These lungs are surrounded by the pleural membranes, which prevent their adhesion to any surrounding tissues. Separating the thoracic cavity from the abdominal cavity below is the diaphragm, upon which the heart and the lungs rest.

410. (D) IgM is an antibody type that can be found in low levels in respiratory secretions, but at nowhere near as high levels as IgA can be found. This is because IgA is synthesized with a special secretory component that conducts it directly through the respiratory epithelial cells and into the mucus.

411. (A) Within the alveolar capillaries (where the air is not quite completely mixed with the atmosphere), the $pO_2 = 100$ mm and the $pCO_2 = 40$ mm. Within the tissues, the $pO_2 = 40$ mm and the $pCO_2 = 45$ mm. This is why O_2 can passively diffuse from the blood into the tissues and why CO_2 leaves the tissues and enters the blood.

412. (B) The receptors responsible for the cough reflex reside in areas for which such a stimulus would be the result of something unexpected or unusual. The oropharynx is the one obvious area listed in which such receptors would be counterproductive. This is because the chewing and swallowing of food would trigger this reflex at every meal, preventing the intake of nutrition.

413. (E) COPD is a serious condition, as impaired gas exchange means decreased oxygenation of peripheral tissues. Options A, B, and D can immediately be excluded, as they are all chronic respiratory conditions. Emphysema is a condition in which the integrity of the alveolar sacs is compromised, which greatly reduces the lung surface areas available for gas exchange. This deterioration is usually gradual and irreversible.

414. (C) Since the air is commonly dry, the mucus membranes in the nose increase the moisture content of the air to prevent the desiccation of the alveoli, and recover those fluids as the air departs again. The convoluted passages in the nose also produce a cyclonic effect that spins debris onto the mucus-coated surfaces for easy removal from the body. An additional benefit is that the olfactory receptors within the nose help steer us away from potentially dangerous putrid or toxic locations or toward a favorite food source.

415. (A) The nephron consists of the glomerulus, Bowman's capsule, and conducting and reabsorption tubules in the order of proximal convoluted tubule, descending tubule, loop of Henle, ascending tubule, distal convoluted tubule, and collecting duct. The blood enters the glomerulus via the afferent arteriole, where it is filtered.

Chapter 11: The Musculoskeletal System

416. (C) In three separate cycles, a rise in curve A precedes a similar rise in curve B. The following pattern of drops in the curves is also consistent. If these data were collected in separate areas, there might be a correlation, but it would be much harder to ascertain. However, if the data were collected in the same geographical areas, a correlation is likely.

417. (B) Assuming that curve A represents the prairie dog population and curve B represents the predator population, then something is happening that produces a rise in the prey population. A rise in the prey population is then followed by a rise in the predator population. The most likely cause of increases in the prey population is increased rainfall, which produces increased growth in the plants used as food by the prairie dog.

418. (A) Applying option A would be most consistent with the data presented. More rain produces more food for the prairie dogs, which increases their numbers in good years. More prairie dogs mean more food for the coyote pups, increasing their numbers. If the rain drops off, this means less food for the prey, dropping their numbers, and then less food for the predators, dropping their numbers.

419. (C) Option A would not be too disruptive as long as the predators were counted consistently, even if the species were combined. Option B would merely produce a small gap in the data but would not damage the observation of the trends. Option D would lower the magnitude of the populations, but would not damage the trends. However, if the rise in predators preceded the rise in prey, some other factor must be considered.

420. (D) A rise in the prey population is followed by a rise in the predator population. The increased predation then causes a drop in the prey population, followed by a drop in the number of predators.

421. (E) Calcium interacts with troponin, which then uncovers myosin binding sites on the tropomyosin strands, which are interwoven along a backbone of actin on the thin filament. This then permits the myosin, which makes up the bulk of the thick filament, to repetitively bind to and detach from the binding sites, producing a walking effect that contracts the sarcomere. All of these components except myosin are thus on the thin filament.

422. (D) If there is a shortfall in calcium release, such as might occur if there is leakage out of the cell, then there can be an insufficient interaction with troponin, resulting in the uncovering of fewer myosin binding sites and resulting in reduced muscle contraction force.

This calcium leakage is known to occur in the elderly, who lose muscle strength even when weight training.

423. (A) The bones are the primary storage location for both phosphate and calcium.

424. (D) Smooth muscle is located throughout the body. Smooth muscle cells are non-striated (that's why they are called smooth). Skeletal muscles are associated with the bony structures of the skeleton. All smooth muscle tissue is under the involuntary control of the autonomic nervous system.

425. (C) The adult human skull is composed of 22 bones. The braincase bones include the ethmoid, frontal, occipital, parietals (2), sphenoid, and temporals (2). The face bones include the volmer, inferior nasal concha, nasal (2), maxilla (2), mandible, palatine, zygomatic (2), and lacrimal.

426. (A) Options B, C, and E indicate muscle pairs that are in opposition, pulling in opposite directions. Option D represents muscles that are on entirely separate limbs.

427. (B) The vertebrae, or bones of the spine, provide support for the remainder of the skeletal structure and protection for the spinal cord. Starting just below the skull, there are seven cervical vertebrae (identified as C1–C7), twelve thoracic vertebrae (T1–T12), five lumbar vertebrae (L1–L5), the five fused bones of the sacrum, and then the three to five fused bones of the coccyx.

428. (A) A joint is defined as a joining between bones. Articulated joints are held in position by ligaments that restrict their range of motion. There are joints, however, that are not intended to be mobile, such as the sutures of the skull. These nonmobile joints are identified as fibrous joints.

429. (E) A sarcomere is the basic contractile unit of the muscle cell and is identified under the microscope as the region of bands located between the Z lines.

430. (B) One of the primary functions of the bones is that they serve as a reservoir for calcium and phosphate, which are vital for organ and cellular function. Long bones are also homes for the tissues that produce blood cells. The skeleton also serves to protect the internal organs from trauma and to provide the support necessary for motion produced by muscle contraction.

431. (B) The sarcoplasmic reticulum serves as a storehouse of calcium ions (Ca^{2+}), a flood of which is necessary to initiate the actin-myosin interactions that produce a muscle contraction.

432. (D) A long bone consists of three broad sections: the two ends, or epiphyses, and the diaphysis in between. The end closest to the head is the proximal epiphysis, and that farthest away is the distal epiphysis. While loss of calcium can lead to osteoporosis, this is an abnormal condition affecting the compact bone and is not related to the normal spongy bone of the epiphyses.

433. (C) The knee is a hinge-joint articulation located between the femur of the upper leg and the tibia and fibia of the lower leg. The tibial layer consists of two disk-shaped cushions known as the lateral and medial meniscus. The menisci are composed of fibrocartilage, not fibrous joining as seen in the skull.

434. (B) Muscle contraction requires a huge expense of energy. The initial supply of ATP on hand is consumed within the first 10 seconds of contraction. After that, the ATP is replenished by the donation of the phosphate group on creatine phosphate to recharge ADP to ATP, which lasts about an additional 30 seconds.

435. (E) Intact compact bone holds two types of cells: osteoplasts, which are free-roving, and osteocytes, which are bone cells that are locked into spaces known as lacuna and connected together by canalicula. Osteoclasts become active within compact bone following a fracture, when they are needed to recycle bone debris. These osteoclasts normally reside in the periosteum.

436. (D) Digestion is under autonomic control. The autonomic nervous system is partially regulated by the brain stem and partially by the spinal cord. The control of peristalsis falls to both branches of the autonomic system, both the sympathetic and parasympathetic systems. So, although options A and C are both true, option D is more complete and is the correct answer.

437. (C) During childhood, spongy bone starts to form at some secondary ossification sites near the ends of the bones. Later, during early adolescence, bone elongation takes place as new cartilage is laid down on the undersurface of the cartilage growth plate, also known as the epiphyseal plate.

438. (E) Joints are held together by collagenous ligaments. This eliminates option D, which does not describe a tendon, although both are composed of collagen, and option B as well. Option C is incorrect because neither of these tissues has an extensive blood supply. Option A describes a synovium sealed within a fibrous joint capsule. It is a tendon that connects bone to muscles.

439. (E) When an action potential signals the need for muscle contraction, it causes a release of calcium ions from the sarcoplasmic reticulum. This calcium interacts with troponin, opening up the myosin binding sites on the tropomyosin strands that cover the thick filament composed of actin. This allows the myosin heads extending from the thin filament to bind to these sites.

440. (C) Neither rheumatoid arthritis nor osteoarthritis affects ligaments. Both can result in permanent deformation. Osteoarthritis is most commonly initiated by a gradual erosion of the intra-articular cartilage until bone starts to grind upon bone, while rheumatoid arthritis is initiated by an inflammatory process that is classified as an autoimmune response.

441. (D) When a myofibril contracts, it is responding to a sudden release of calcium ions from the sarcoplasmic reticulum, which then permits the expenditure of ATP to activate the sliding filament mechanism that produces muscle contraction. The ions dumped in one cell rapidly pass to adjacent cells through the connecting gap junctions, producing a synchronized beating.

442. (E) When a bone fractures, blood flows out of the vessels in the haversian canals and produces a clot, or hematoma, that fills the fractured area. A fibrocartilage superstructure is then formed between the bone ends to immobilize them within the resulting callus. Osteo-clasts start dissolving the damaged crystalline structure for recycling. Following behind their hollow trail are osteoblasts that deposit fresh reformed bone.

443. (C) The spaces between the ribs are known as intercostal spaces; intervertebral spaces are filled by the intervertebral disks between the vertebrae.

444. (A) Tendons attach to bones that are relatively immobile at points known as origins, and attach to bones that are designed to move when the muscle contracts at points called insertions. This means that insertions are pulled toward origins.

445. (E) The skeleton is divided into two parts: the axial skeleton, which runs along the midline from the skull to the coccyx and includes the rib cage, and the appendicular skel-eton, which rests upon the axial skeleton. If a bone is not within the midline, then it is part of the appendicular portion.

446. (A) After about 45 seconds of exertion, in order to fuel additional muscle contraction, glucose must be released from glycogen stores in the liver. If there are no glycogen stores, such as in McArdle's disease, then the muscles lose their ability to contract after very little effort.

447. (B) The tibia and fibula are the two bones that stand parallel to each other in the lower leg, running between the knee and the tarsal bones of the foot. Analogous to these are the radius and ulna, the two bones that stand parallel to each other in the lower arm, running from the elbow to the carpal bones of the hand.

448. (D) Osteoporosis is a condition brought on by calcium depletion within the compact bone. Trying to increase calcium blood levels is a reasonable way to try to replenish bone mass caused by calcium loss, and moderate exercise or stretching to slightly increase stress, and thus bone strength in response, is also a common approach to treating this condition.

449. (A) The latissimus dorsi contract to draw the arms backward and downward toward the body. The gluteus maximus extends the thighs and rotates them laterally. The external obliques rotate the trunk and squeeze the abdomen. The serratus anterior draw the shoulder blades forward and help raise the arms. The rectus abdominis is the muscle group used for bending the spine forward, as in a sit-up.

450. (C) The spine normally curves both ventrally and dorsally. However, lateral curves, especially when excessive, can produce the symptoms of scoliosis: difficulty breathing, con-tinued degeneration of the spine, severe chronic pain or numbness, and disfigurement. This condition may be identified in childhood, may not develop or be noticed until adolescence, or may appear in adulthood.

451. (E) Normal long bone development starts with the formation of an initial bone-shaped structure that acts like a mold formed of cartilage. Inside this form, ossification takes place from the center outward, but some of the original cartilage is retained near the ends. Another term for this is endochondrial bone.

452. (B) When large amounts of energy are expended producing the muscle exertion during exercise, larger than normal amounts of oxygen must be available to permit a maximum level of ATP production. Commonly, the respiratory and circulatory systems are incapable of providing adequate amounts of oxygen. Thus, cells switch from the much more efficient oxidative phosphorylation to fermentation, with a resulting buildup of lactic acid in the muscles. Once the exertion ceases, oxygenation must remain high in order to allow the conversion of the lactic acid back into glucose and the restoration of creatine phosphate and ATP to normal levels.

453. (C) All protein function is dependent on protein shape, which, in turn, is dependent on the physiologic conditions in which it is present. Thus, in order to maintain homeostasis and all body functions, physiologic conditions must be maintained within a narrow range. This includes fluid and electrolyte balance and temperature.

454. (A) Atrial natriuretic peptide (ANP) is involved in decreasing blood pressure and increasing vasodilation. Cholecystokinin (CCK) is involved in digestion and the sense of satiety. Inflammatory prostaglandins are produced by cells that have suffered traumatic damage. When the kidneys detect poor oxygenation of the blood, much as might occur when someone moves to a higher altitude, they release erythropoietin (EPO) to stimulate the bone marrow to a higher rate of erythrocyte production.

455. (D) Skeletal muscle is subdivided into two broad categories: fast twitch and slow twitch. Fast-twitch muscle contracts more rapidly and with greater force than slow-twitch muscle, but tires more quickly. Slow-twitch muscle has a higher density of myoglobin and mitochondria and a richer capillary bed, thus making it redder than fast-twitch muscle. Additionally, slow-twitch muscle is capable of more sustained but weaker contraction than fast-twitch.

456. (B) The cytochromes of the electron transport system were first discovered in insect muscles. This was because their extremely high metabolic rate was due to a very high density of mitochondria, making such studies easier. It is thought by researchers that, because insects are cold-blooded, the constant motion is necessary to keep the muscles warm enough for immediate use.

457. (C) When a physician taps the patellar tendon with a rubber hammer, the resulting sudden stretching of the knee extensor muscle triggers a reflex that causes the lower leg to extend suddenly. This is a response when the body senses what it interprets as the sudden collapse of the leg and an anticipated resulting loss of an upright body position. This myotatic response is also known as the knee-jerk, stretch, or deep tendon reflex. A flexor reflex is a response to a skin receptor's detection of pain, such as a nail in the foot or a hand on a hot pan.

458. (E) Actin is most closely associated with muscle contraction and the cytoskeleton framework. Keratin is the major structural protein of fully differentiated skin cells, hair, and nails. Fibronectin, best associated with blood and the extracellular matrix, and elastin, best associated with tissues subject to stretching forces, such as arteries and veins, are both major components of connective tissue. However, it is collagen that comprises up to 30 percent of a bone's mass, the remainder being inorganic hydroxyapatite.

Chapter 12: Reproduction and Development

459. (A) Monoecious is a term used by botanists to describe a single plant that has both male and female gonads. This would therefore be an incorrect use of this term, so option D is out. Selection is a process, so option E can also be ignored. Polymorphism means "many shapes," but the term is used in biology to describe phenotypic variations that lead to diversity, not differences in sexual morphology. This makes option C a poor choice. Males and females may have features that distinguish them from the other sex, but the presence of those features within a population is referred to as sexual dimorphism, making option A the preferred choice.

460. (B) An ectopic pregnancy is one in which the blastocyst attempts implantation at some location other than in the uterus. This attempt may be on the peritoneal lining, ovaries, or cervix, but the most common location is within the fallopian tube itself. Thus, it is described as a tubal pregnancy; these account for 95 percent of such pregnancies.

461. (D) In spermatogenesis, the spermatogonium divides by mitosis. Upon dividing, the cell that is in contact with the seminiferous tubule remains to divide again, while the one that is closer to the lumen (the diploid primary spermatocyte) undergoes meiosis. It first replicates its chromosomes to become tetraploid, then undergoes meiosis I to become two diploid secondary spermatocytes, and then immediately undergoes meiosis II to become four spermatids.

462. (B) A woman's reproductive age runs from the onset of menses at about age 15 to menopause at about age 55, for a total of about 40 years. One or two eggs mature and are released every 28 days or so. This means that a total of about 500 eggs become available for fertilization during a woman's reproductive lifetime. Estimates for the total number of eggs produced within the ovaries before birth range from 500,000 to 1,500,000.

463. (C) Each oocyte undergoes asymmetrical cell division, so that only one of the four resulting haploid cells contains the bulk of the original cell mass and nutrients. During the formation of the mature ovum, the primary oocyte undergoes meiosis I to produce a secondary oocyte and one smaller-sized polar body. After both cells undergo meiosis II, there remains one haploid ovum and three much smaller haploid polar bodies.

464. (B) The male reproductive system contains various tissues with different functions. Sperm are formed in the seminiferous tubules that make up the bulk of the testes.

465. (A) The ovarian cycle consists of the follicular phase (days 1–14), during which FSH levels rise and the maturing ovarian follicle containing the secondary oocyte increases estrogen and progesterone levels, and the luteal phase, when LH levels rise, causing the release of the oocyte, and the residual corpus luteum starts secreting progesterone.

466. (C) A human sperm is a greatly reduced haploid cell. The sperm itself is composed of a head covered with the acrosome and containing the nucleus. While the description given in option B may be true (although we do not know that), we do know that option C is true, making it the best choice.

467. (C) What is not seen in any sperm is any significant amount of cytosol, and since the sperm has no mission other than to fertilize the ovum, it has no need for protein synthesis, which eliminates the need for an endoplasmic reticulum, Golgi apparatus, or ribosomes.

468. (E) Sertoli cells serve to support spermatogenesis by clearing the cytoplasmic debris released during sperm maturation and to secrete various substances that work with or on testosterone, but not the testosterone itself, which is the responsibility of the seminiferous tubule interstitial cells.

469. (E) Oxytocin is responsible for expelling the milk from the alveoli in which it is produced. The presence of estrogen at high levels following delivery slows milk production. The sudden drop in progesterone level induces milk production following delivery. Prolactin is responsible for regulating milk production following birth. Testosterone has no role in lactation.

470. (B) Both the luteal phase of the ovarian cycle and the secretory phase of the uterine cycle occur between days 15 and 28 of the menstrual cycle.

471. (E) Options A–D are all components of the human male reproduction system. The ureters are the tubes that connect the kidneys to the urinary bladder.

472. (D) Both FSH and LH are vital in the formation of seminiferous tubules and testosterone, respectively, and are produced within the anterior pituitary. The hypothalamus controls the anterior pituitary by producing a gonadotropin-releasing hormone.

473. (B) Oogenesis, the formation of the mature ovum, is a process that follows the normal meiotic pathway, with the tetraploid primary oocyte dividing into two diploid cells, which then further divide into four haploid gametes. What distinguishes the resulting three polar bodies from the single ovum is the unequal distribution of cytoplasm, not DNA.

474. (A) Yes, the Pap smear is old, but it is still the best screen for cervical cancer. While the PCR for HPV is more sensitive, and can be highly specific for the high-risk genotypes that are most linked to cancer, if the virus is detected without any evidence of dysplasia, the treatment plan is to wait and periodically follow up with . . . the Pap smear.

475. (D) Endometriosis is a problem associated with scarring of the oviducts or ovaries, but the most common symptom is pelvic pain. While scarring may be the cause, the degree of infertility is not related to the degree of scarring. The precise cause is still unknown.

476. (A) Preembryonic development begins only after fertilization of the secondary oocyte by the sperm. After fertilization, the now diploid cell divides three times without intervening growth periods, ending this cleavage period with eight cells, but with a total mass equal to the zygote. These cells then begin growing and increasing in numbers as the morula continues passing down the fallopian tube to the uterus. The final stage, the blastocyst, is advanced enough for implantation into the uterine wall.

477. (E) The cells on the exterior of the blastula form the ectoderm, the inner sphere forms the endoderm, and the connections between them form the mesoderm. The ectoderm will then undergo differentiation, forming the nervous system (including the posterior pituitary and the retina of the eye), the epidermis, and tissues associated with the epidermis, such as sweat glands, the lining of the mouth, and tooth enamel. The functioning portions of the thymus are formed from the endoderm.

478. (A) The formation of a vertebrate's central nervous system follows the formation of the notochord because the notochord establishes the developmental axis of the organism. When the notochord has begun forming, then the adjacent neural plate forms on its ventral side. This plate then forms a furrow or groove, invaginates further to form a fold, and then spreads open its interior to form the neural tube.

479. (D) The allantois, which includes the chorion, is a tissue associated with the handling of liquid fetal waste and eventually gives rise to the urinary bladder.

480. (D) Option E can be eliminated because an unfertilized ovum is incapable of further division. Option A is also not possible because of the change in the zygote cell membrane that occurs immediately after fertilization. Option B would result in genetically related but distinct fraternal twins. Option C has been known to occur and results in a chimeric, or tetragametic, individual who appears normal, but who possesses cells with different genetic content.

481. (A) From the mesoderm layer develop muscle tissues and connective tissues, which include the bone marrow, from which all blood components derive, and the circulatory and lymph systems.

482. (B) The neural crest originates from the ectoderm germ line, but it has often been referred to as a fourth line because it is the source of many widely dispersed differentiated cells. These cells include neural and glial cells, medulla cells of the adrenal glands, skeletal and various connective tissues of the head, and pigment-producing cells of the skin.

483. (E) Both the fingers of the hand and the toes of the feet are initially connected by this extra tissue. However, prior to birth, these cells are removed by apoptosis, and the digits are normally fully separated. In some cases, however, the apoptotic process is not complete, and some digits remain fully or partially connected. This condition is called syndactyly and it is an autosomal recessive trait.

484. (C) Infant jaundice is caused when a mother's naturally forming anti-blood group antibodies cross the placenta and damage some of the infant's red blood cells in cases of an ABO mismatch. This destruction releases bilirubin, which is observed as the yellowish skin and eye condition known as jaundice.

485. (C) During very early embryonic development, three basic germ layers form, from which all future tissues and organs develop. From the endoderm develop the bulk of the gastrointestinal system, the liver, pancreas, lungs, thymus and thyroid glands, portions of the ears, and the urinary bladder.

486. (B) Cellular differentiation during development always depends on specific signals given off by nearby cells that produce a specific response in receptive cells. In order for the cell to respond to any signal, it must have a specific receptor for that signal, the signal/receptor complex must produce a response at the transcription level, and the resulting translated protein must have some regulatory effect by either stimulating or repressing some gene expression that follows.

487. (E) Since to the mother's immune system, the fetal tissues represent a foreign object with distinctly different antigens, the placenta also provides a barrier that protects the fetus from maternal rejection. However, an infant is protected for a few months after delivery by serum antibodies acquired from the mother during gestation.

488. (B) Mammals, along with birds and reptiles, produce four extraembryonic membranes that support fetal development: the amnion, the allantois, the yolk sac, and the chorion. The myometrium is maternal, not fetal, tissue and is responsible for uterine contraction during childbirth.

489. (B) During the first three weeks of gestation, the embryo undergoes first initial tissue differentiation, then gastrulation, which results in the formation of the three initial germ layers: the ectoderm, mesoderm, and endoderm. During the fourth week, the eyes appear, the limbs and bones begin to form, and the heart begins to beat.

490. (D) The tissues between the fingers and toes are initially vasculated, but the blood vessels disappear at the same time as the tissues themselves. While option C may present a plausible explanation, option D is the actual correct choice.

491. (A) During embryonic development, the initial cell mass becomes a hollow ball called a blastula, a stage that all animals have. Some animals, such as a jellyfish, develop a single opening that functions as both mouth and anus. The sphere with its opening structure is a gastrula, and this single opening is known as a blind gut. Other animals develop two openings that function separately as mouth and anus. In protostomes, such as insects, the mouth opening develops first. In deuterostomes, such as mammals, the anus develops first.

492. (E) Epithelium is used to describe tissues that serve primarily as lining or separation barriers. Squamous is used to describe cells that are flat and thin, much like the shape of a shield. Keratin is a protein that is designed to provide an impenetrable barrier. Epithelial tissues composed of overlapping shieldlike squamous cells that contain keratin function best as a barrier that allows nothing to get in and nothing to get out, as in the skin.

493. (C) Goblet cells are found in the epithelial lining of organs. These cells secrete mucin. Mucus (hydrated mucin) functions as a lubricant and as a component associated with protecting surfaces from microbial invasion by trapping microorganisms and dust. These cells are thus found in the trachea and bronchioles of the lungs, in the luminal lining of the small and large intestines, and in the conjunctiva of the eyes, but not in the kidneys.

494. (A) The structures listed in this question are cell-to-cell joining structures. They are best associated with very tight adhesions, which are usually present to prevent cell separation caused by high abrasion conditions. Skin is subject to all sorts of abuse and abrasions that would shred the tissues if they were loosely connected.

495. (E) Blastula formation begins near the 128-cell stage, when cell size and the rate of cellular division begin to normalize. It is also near this stage that the cells first begin to interconnect, with the formation of tight junctions that begin the process of polar orientation and the start of the differentiation of primordial tissues.

496. (C) The human conceptus, from the Latin word for zygote, consists of the newly formed embryo and associated membranes and derivatives, which include the yolk sac, chorion, amnion, and embryonic portions of the placenta. The umbilical cord does not form until after implantation and the formation of the maternal placenta.

497. (B) Fertilization within the fallopian tube normally takes place within a day or so of ovulation. By around day 4, the morula cell mass enters the uterus, and the blastocyst stage implants around day 9, plus or minus two or three days.

498. (D) While the cause is uncertain, on rare occasions, a fertilization event results in either a haploid or a triploid zygote. While this cell will grow, divide, and adhere to the uterine wall, and may even initiate the production of βHCG, mimicking a true pregnancy, the growth will not differentiate properly and is nonviable. More infrequently, the cell mass may become invasive and need to be treated as a cancerous growth.

499. (E) A child's cells, not just its DNA, can be detected in mothers decades following childbirth. These cells seem to be undifferentiated stem cells that can possibly precipitate some autoimmune disorders, such as lupus or scleroderma, but have also been found present and differentiating into replacement neurons in the mother's brain. Both the mother's and child's cells can cross the placenta, and as much as 1 in 100 of fetal cells may be from the mother at an early point in gestation. This implies that all humans are microchimeric individuals.

500. (A) Maternal twins are the result of a single fertilization event, but with early complete partition of the original cell mass before implantation. They have identical genomes. Fraternal twins are the result of two separate fertilization events (separate ova are fertilized almost simultaneously by separate sperm). They have unique genomes and can even be from different fathers. Conjoined (or siamese) twins are the result of a single fertilization event, but with incomplete partition into identical individuals. There are rare cases of an early fusion of fraternal twin cell masses resulting in individuals being composed of cells from two once-separate individuals (from four gametes), and even having cells that are one-half male and one-half female mixed thoroughly or even bilaterally.